STILL CREATING

THE DIARY FOR INVENTORS AND THEIR WORKS

Activinotes

Activinotes

DAILY JOURNALS, PLANNERS, NOTEBOOKS AND OTHER BLANK BOOKS

_____

Inventor's Name

_____

Address

_____

Contact Number

_____

Email Address

INVENTION NAME

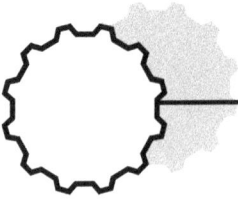

_____

- Function _____

_____

- How did you come up with the invention

_____

_____

- Importance of the Invention _____

_____

_____

Illustration of the Invention

FORMULAS & ROUGH SKETCHES

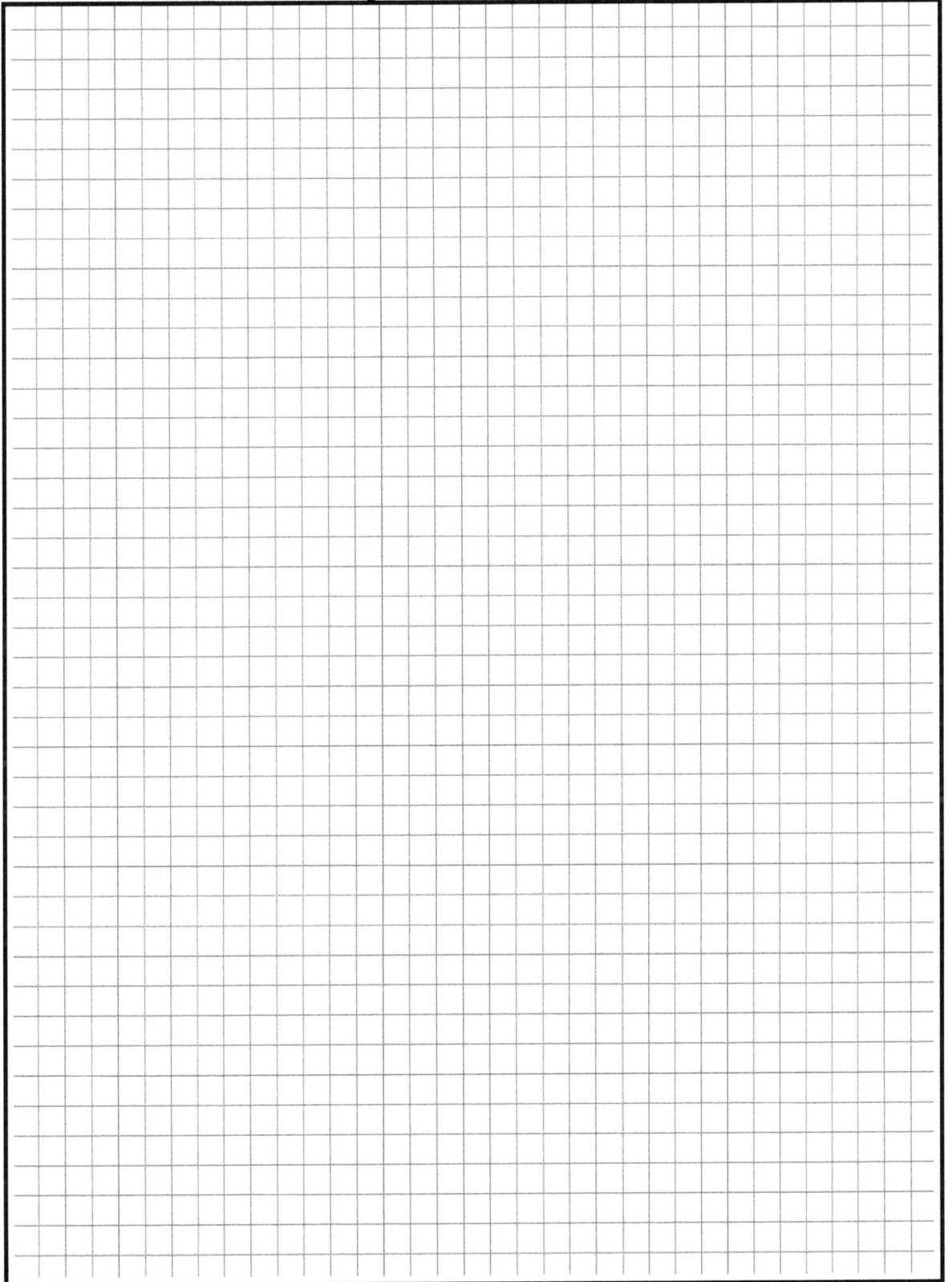

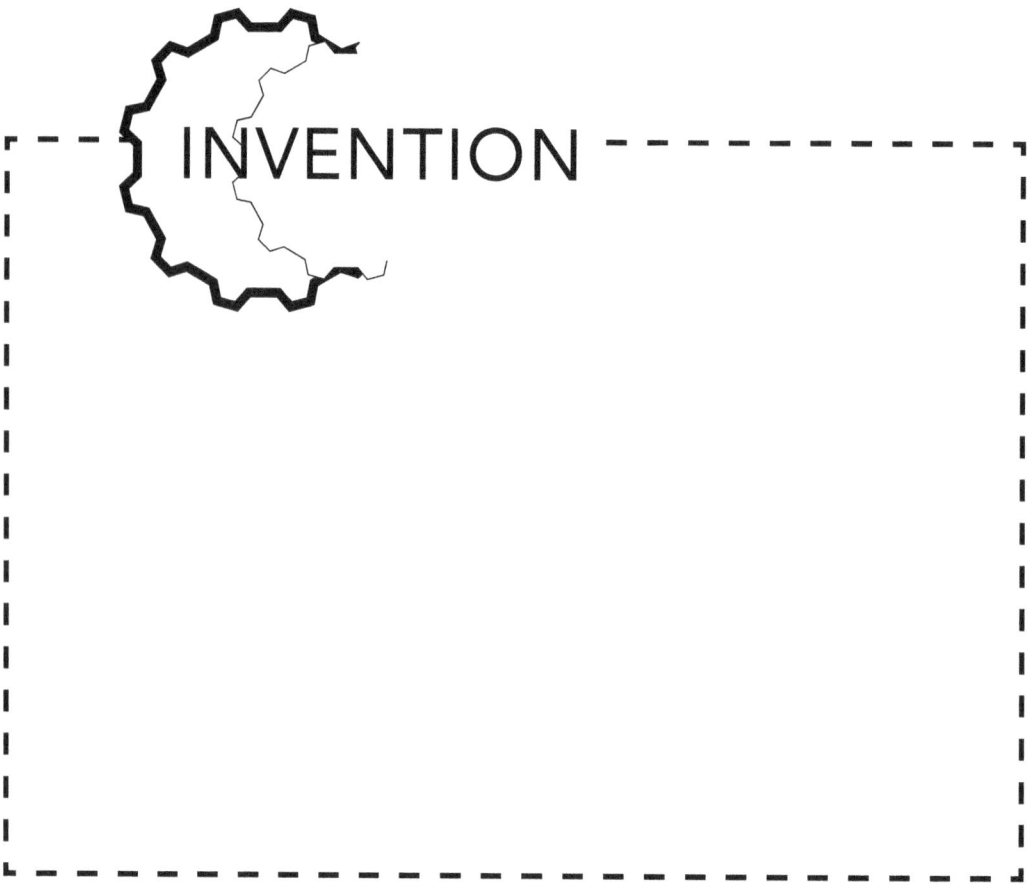

INVENTION

Description: _____
_____
_____

Designed / Created by: _____

Date created: _____

Where created: _____

Significance: _____
_____
_____

INVENTION NAME

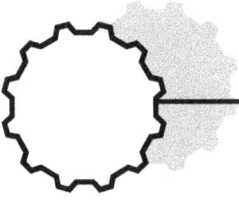

_____

- Function _____
_____

- How did you come up with the invention
_____
_____

- Importance of the Invention _____
_____
_____

Illustration of the Invention

FORMULAS & ROUGH SKETCHES

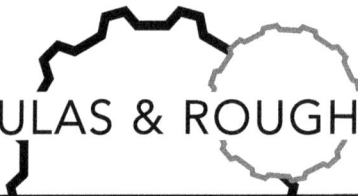

INVENTION

Description: _____

_____

_____

Designed / Created by: _____

Date created: _____

Where created: _____

Significance: _____

_____

_____

INVENTION NAME

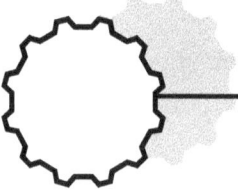

_____

- Function _____
_____

- How did you come up with the invention
_____
_____

- Importance of the Invention _____
_____
_____

Illustration of the Invention

FORMULAS & ROUGH SKETCHES

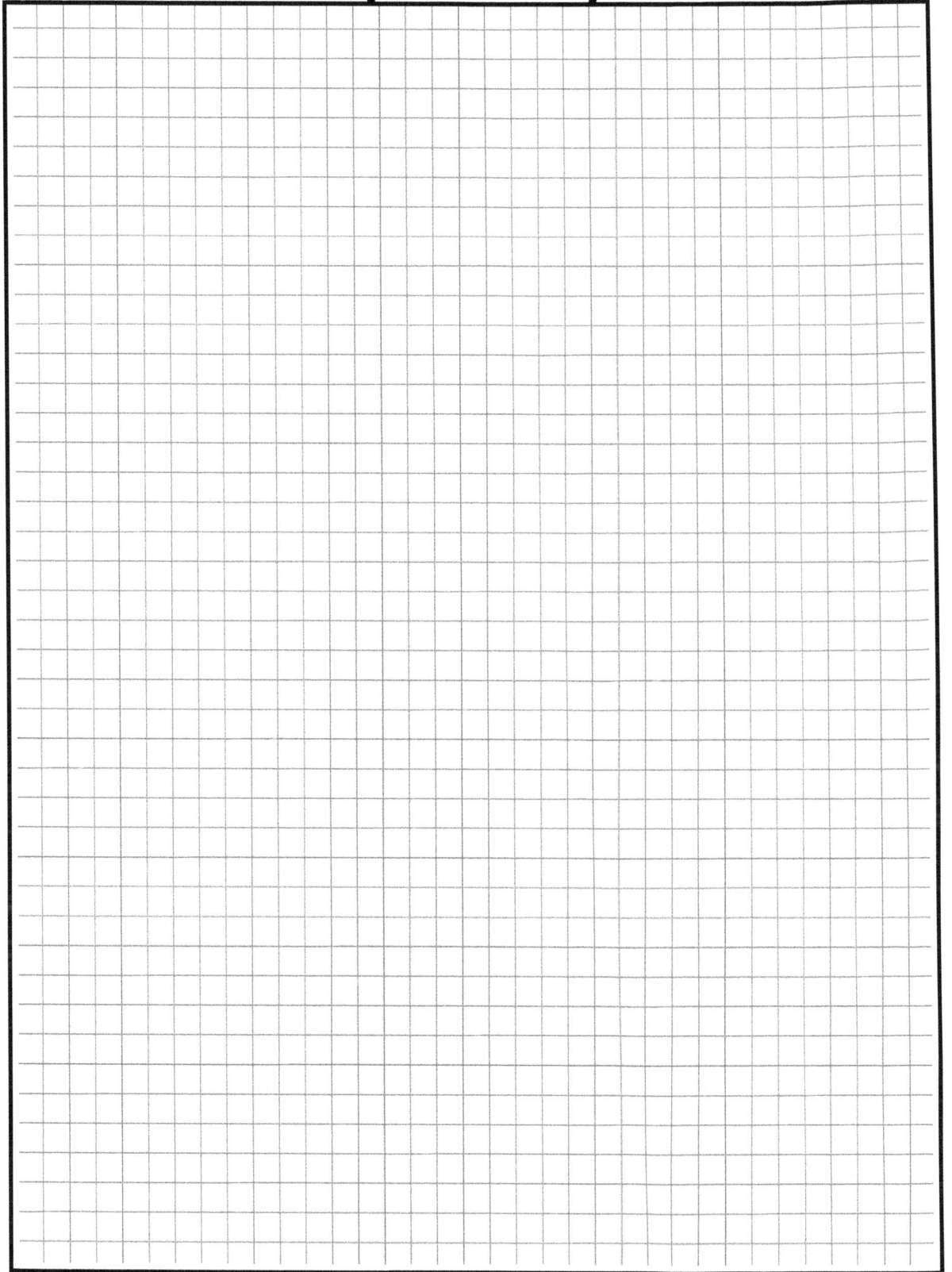

INVENTION

Description: _____
_____
_____

Designed / Created by: _____

Date created: _____

Where created: _____

Significance: _____
_____
_____

FORMULAS & ROUGH SKETCHES

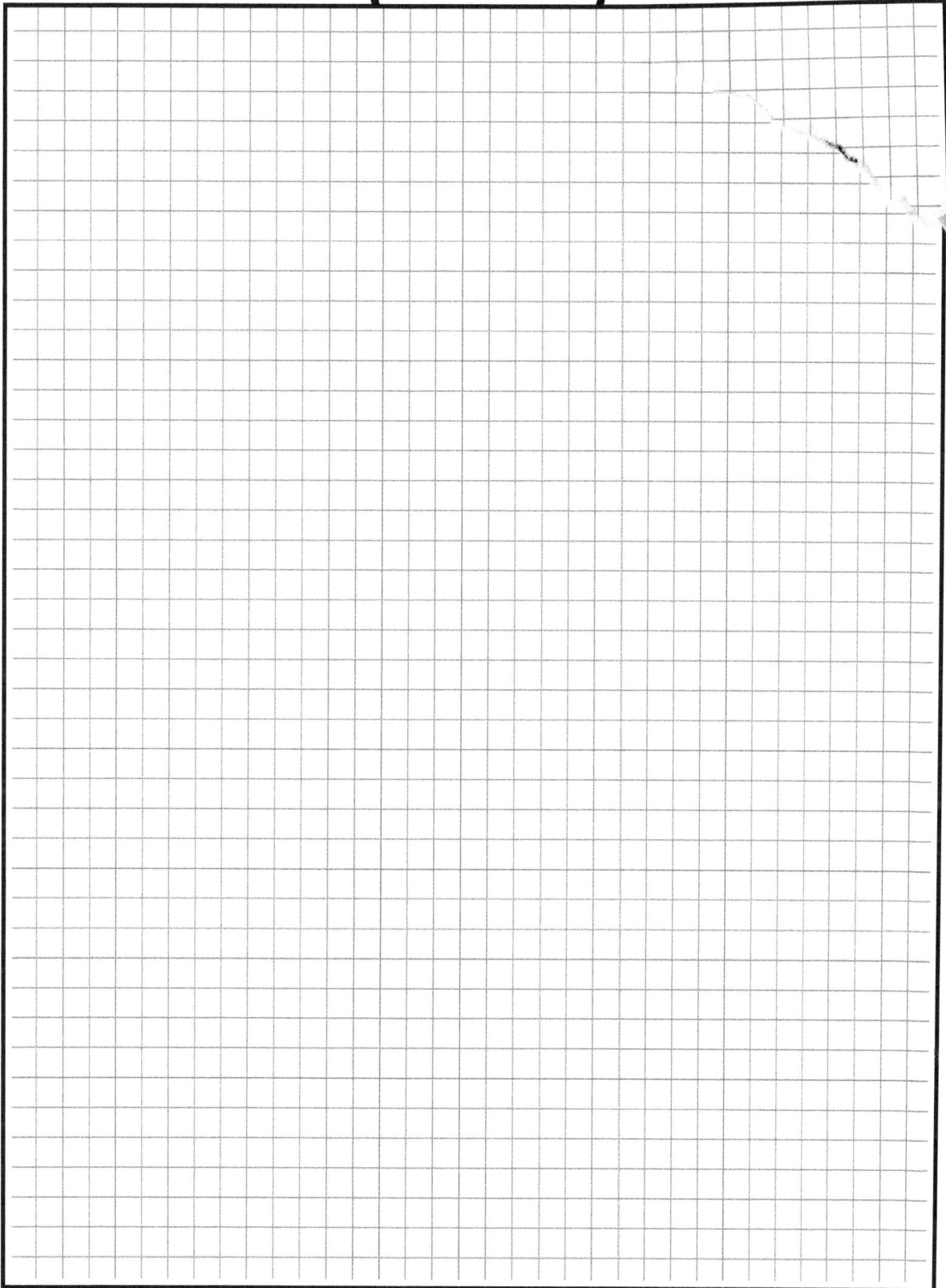

INVENTION NAME

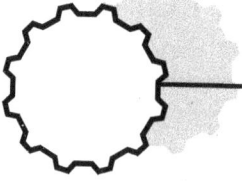

_____

- Function _____
_____

- How did you come up with the invention
_____
_____

- Importance of the Invention _____
_____
_____

Illustration of the Invention

INVENTION

Description: _____

_____

_____

Designed / Created by: _____

Date created: _____

Where created: _____

Significance: _____

_____

_____

INVENTION NAME

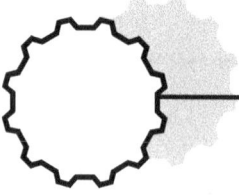

○ _____

• Function _____
_____

• How did you come up with the invention
_____
_____

• Importance of the Invention _____
_____
_____

Illustration of the Invention

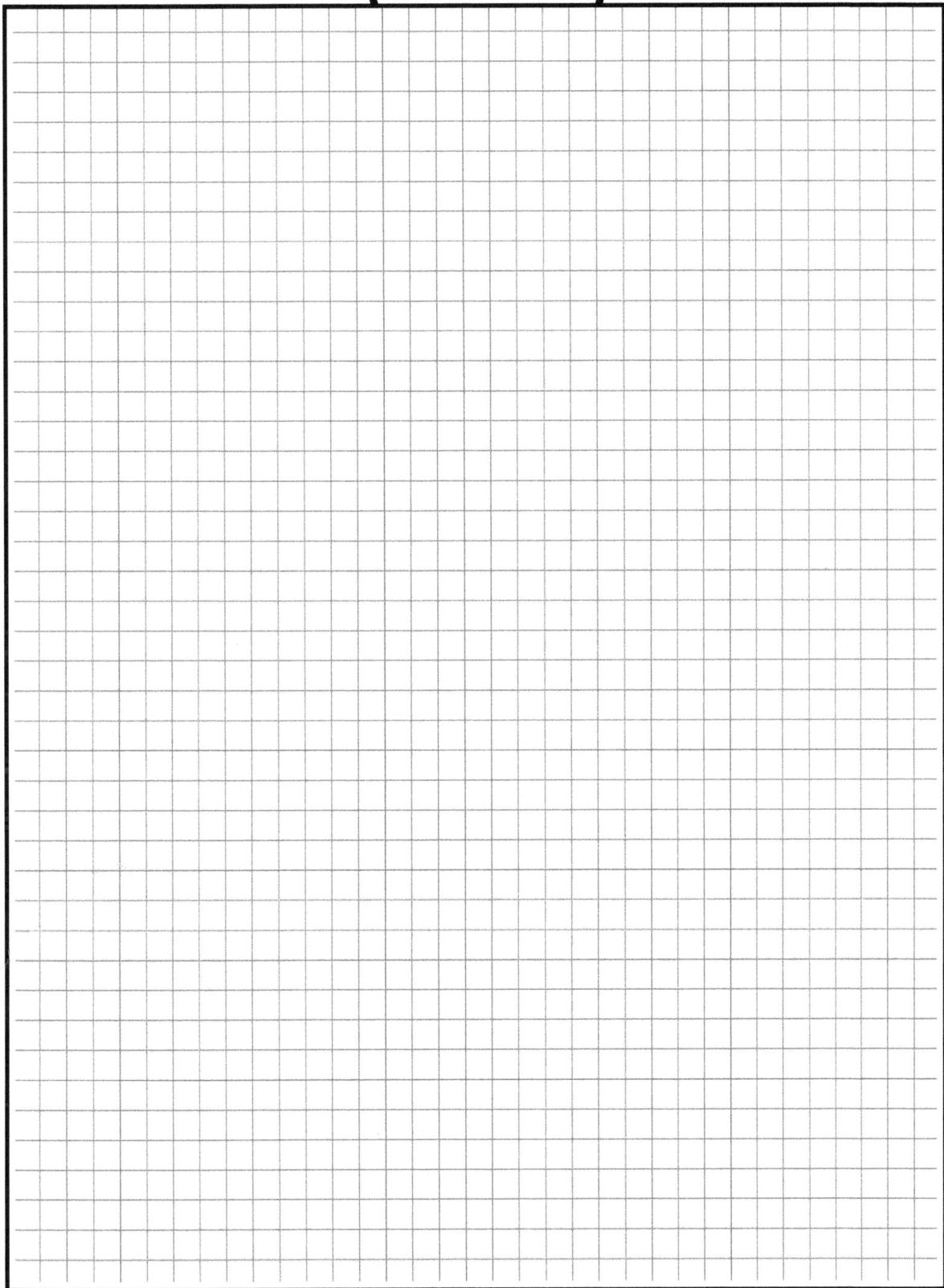

INVENTION

Description: _____

_____

_____

Designed / Created by: _____

Date created: _____

Where created: _____

Significance: _____

_____

_____

INVENTION NAME

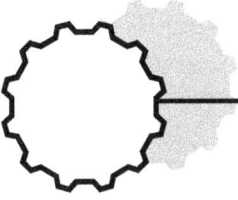

_____

- Function _____
_____

- How did you come up with the invention

_____
_____

- Importance of the Invention _____
_____
_____

Illustration of the Invention

FORMULAS & ROUGH SKETCHES

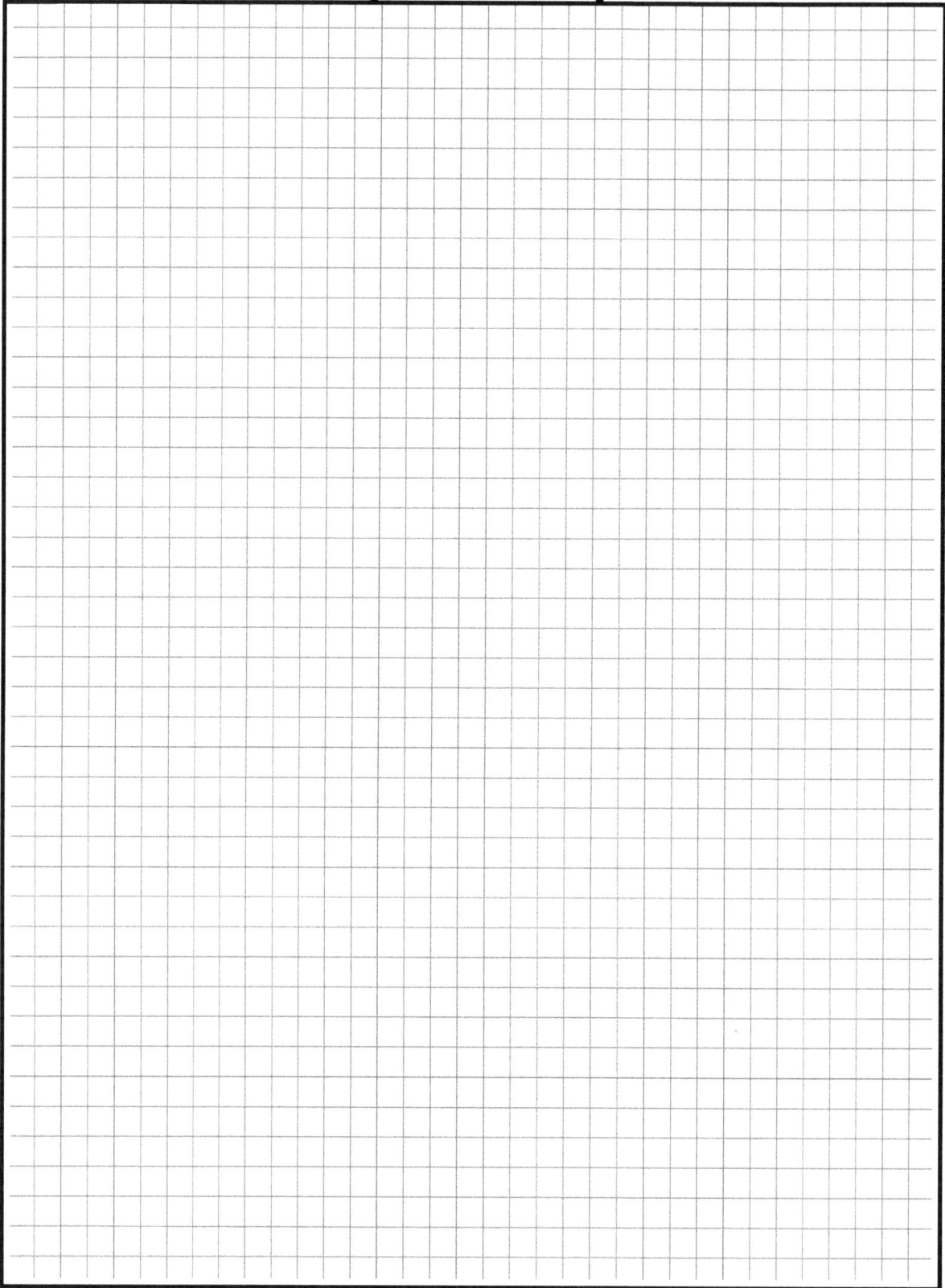

INVENTION

Description: _____
_____
_____

Designed / Created by: _____

Date created: _____

Where created: _____

Significance: _____
_____
_____

INVENTION NAME

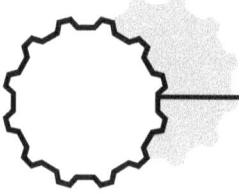

_____

- Function _____
_____

- How did you come up with the invention
_____
_____

- Importance of the Invention _____
_____
_____

Illustration of the Invention

FORMULAS & ROUGH SKETCHES

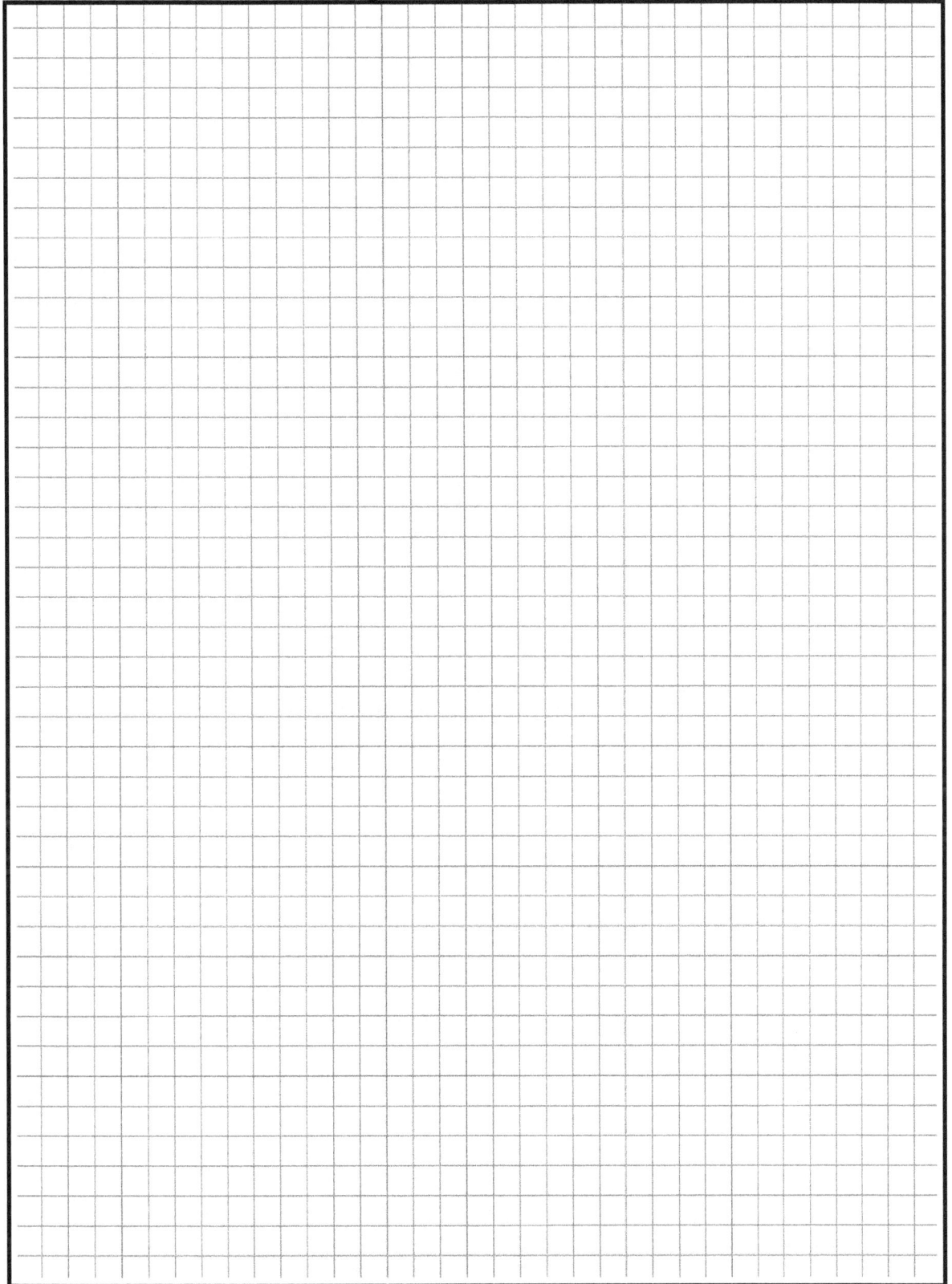

INVENTION

Description: _____

_____

_____

Designed / Created by: _____

Date created: _____

Where created: _____

Significance: _____

_____

_____

INVENTION NAME

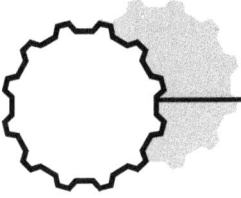

_____

- Function _____
_____

- How did you come up with the invention
_____
_____

- Importance of the Invention _____
_____
_____

Illustration of the Invention

FORMULAS & ROUGH SKETCHES

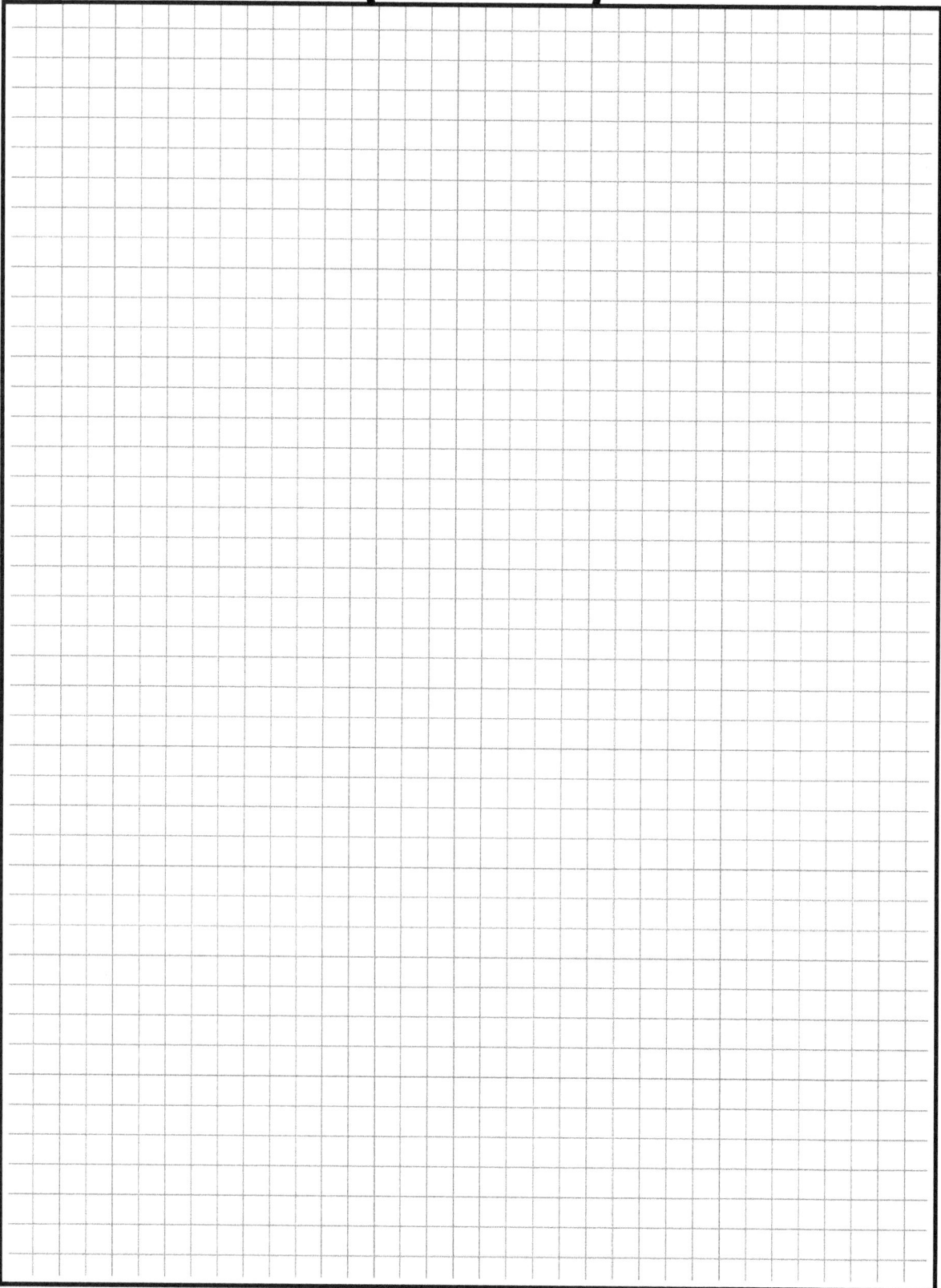

INVENTION

Description: _____
_____
_____

Designed / Created by: _____

Date created: _____

Where created: _____

Significance: _____
_____
_____

INVENTION NAME

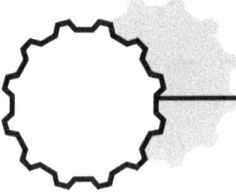

_____

• Function _____
_____

• How did you come up with the invention
_____
_____

• Importance of the Invention _____
_____
_____

Illustration of the Invention

FORMULAS & ROUGH SKETCHES

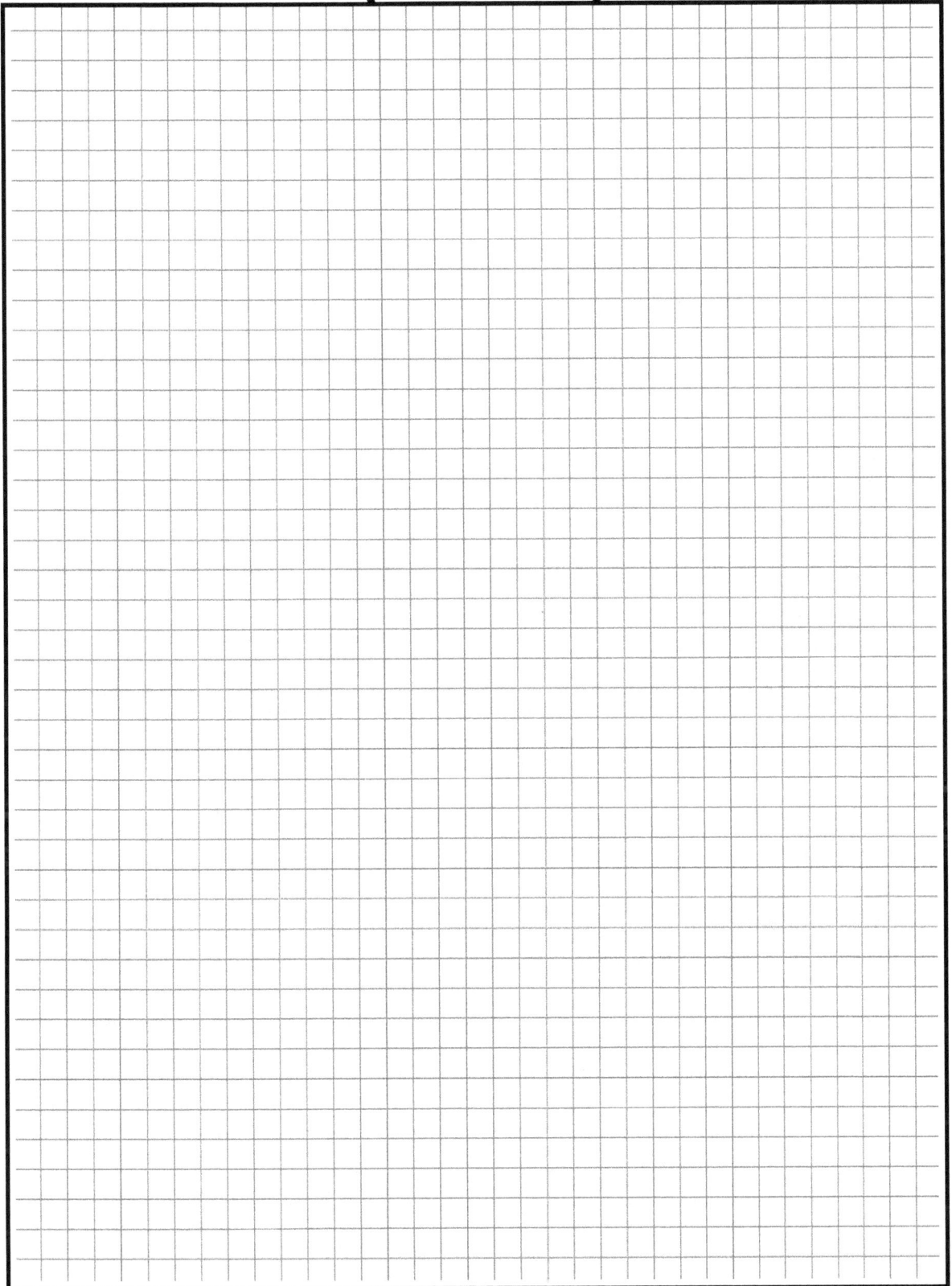

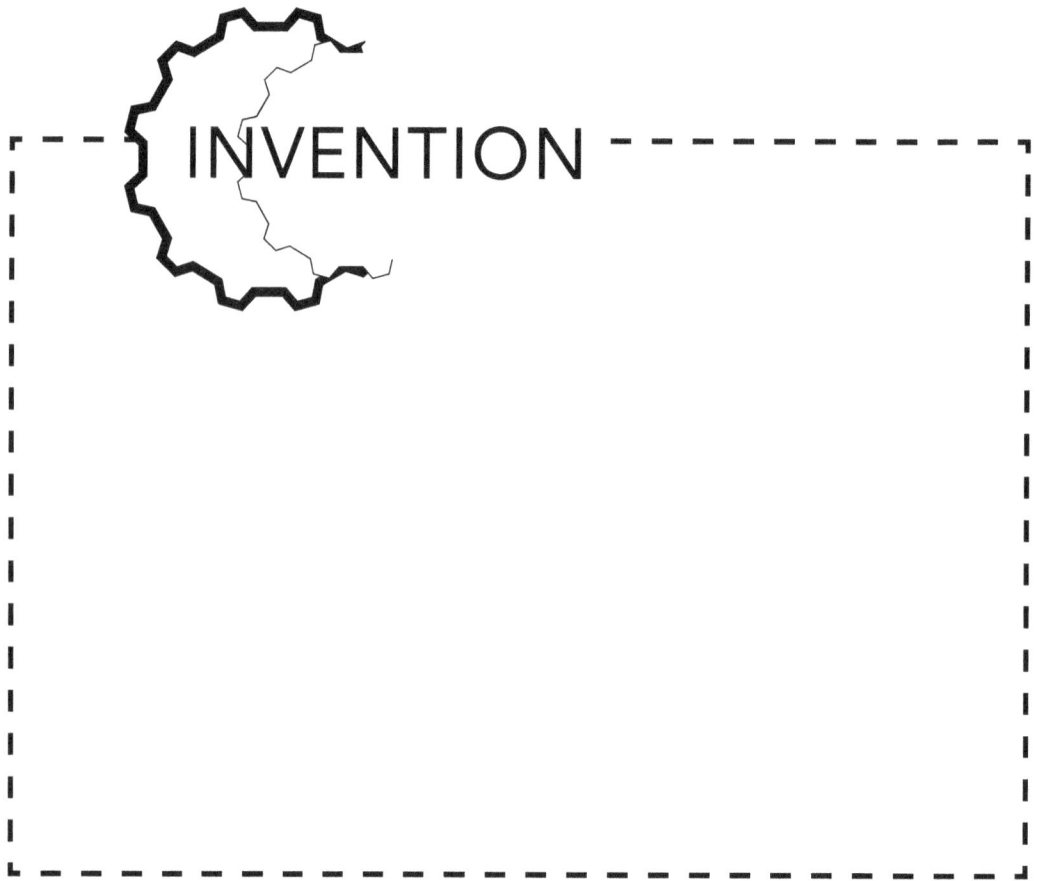

INVENTION

Description: _____

_____

_____

Designed / Created by: _____

Date created: _____

Where created: _____

Significance: _____

_____

_____

INVENTION NAME

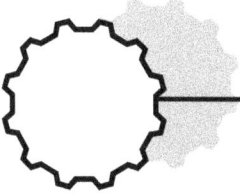

_____

- Function _____
_____

- How did you come up with the invention
_____
_____

- Importance of the Invention _____
_____
_____

Illustration of the Invention

FORMULAS & ROUGH SKETCHES

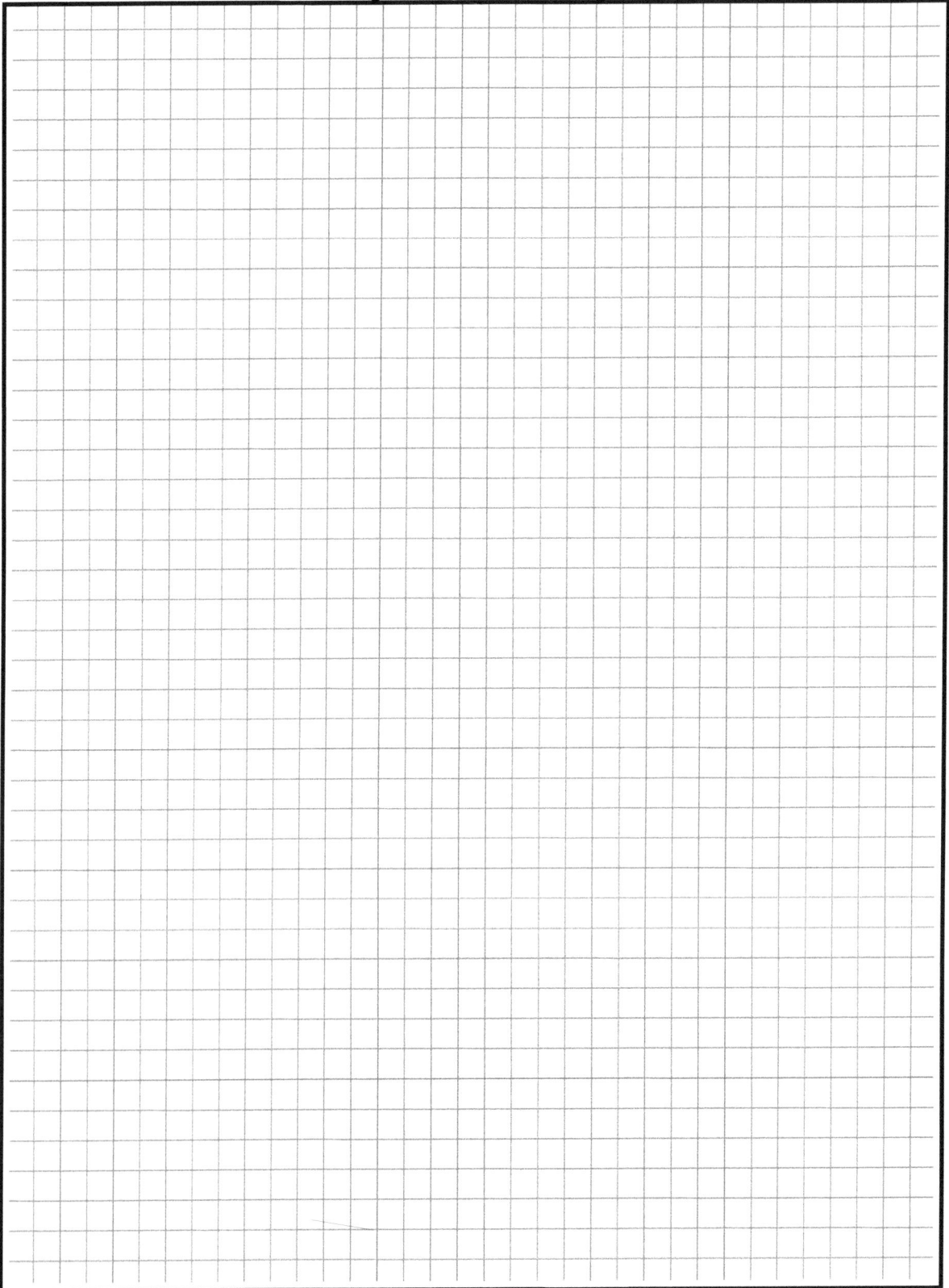

INVENTION

Description: _____

_____

_____

Designed / Created by: _____

Date created: _____

Where created: _____

Significance: _____

_____

_____

INVENTION NAME

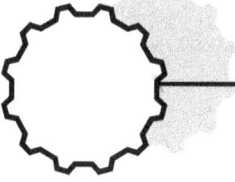

_____

- Function _____
_____

- How did you come up with the invention
_____
_____

- Importance of the Invention _____
_____
_____

Illustration of the Invention

FORMULAS & ROUGH SKETCHES

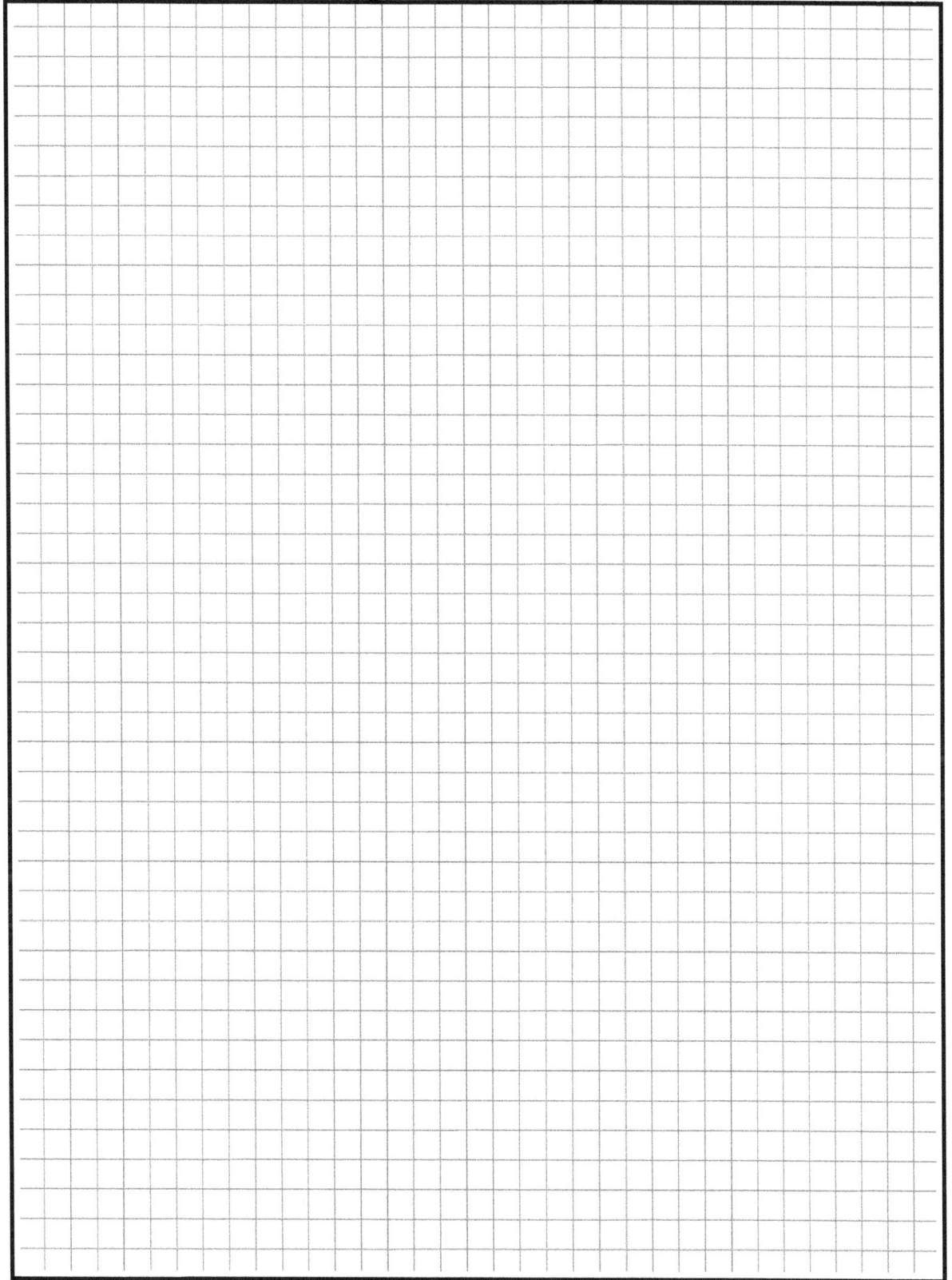

INVENTION

Description: _____

_____

_____

Designed / Created by: _____

Date created: _____

Where created: _____

Significance: _____

_____

_____

INVENTION NAME

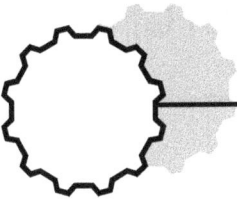

_____

- Function _____
_____

- How did you come up with the invention
_____
_____

- Importance of the Invention _____
_____
_____

Illustration of the Invention

FORMULAS & ROUGH SKETCHES

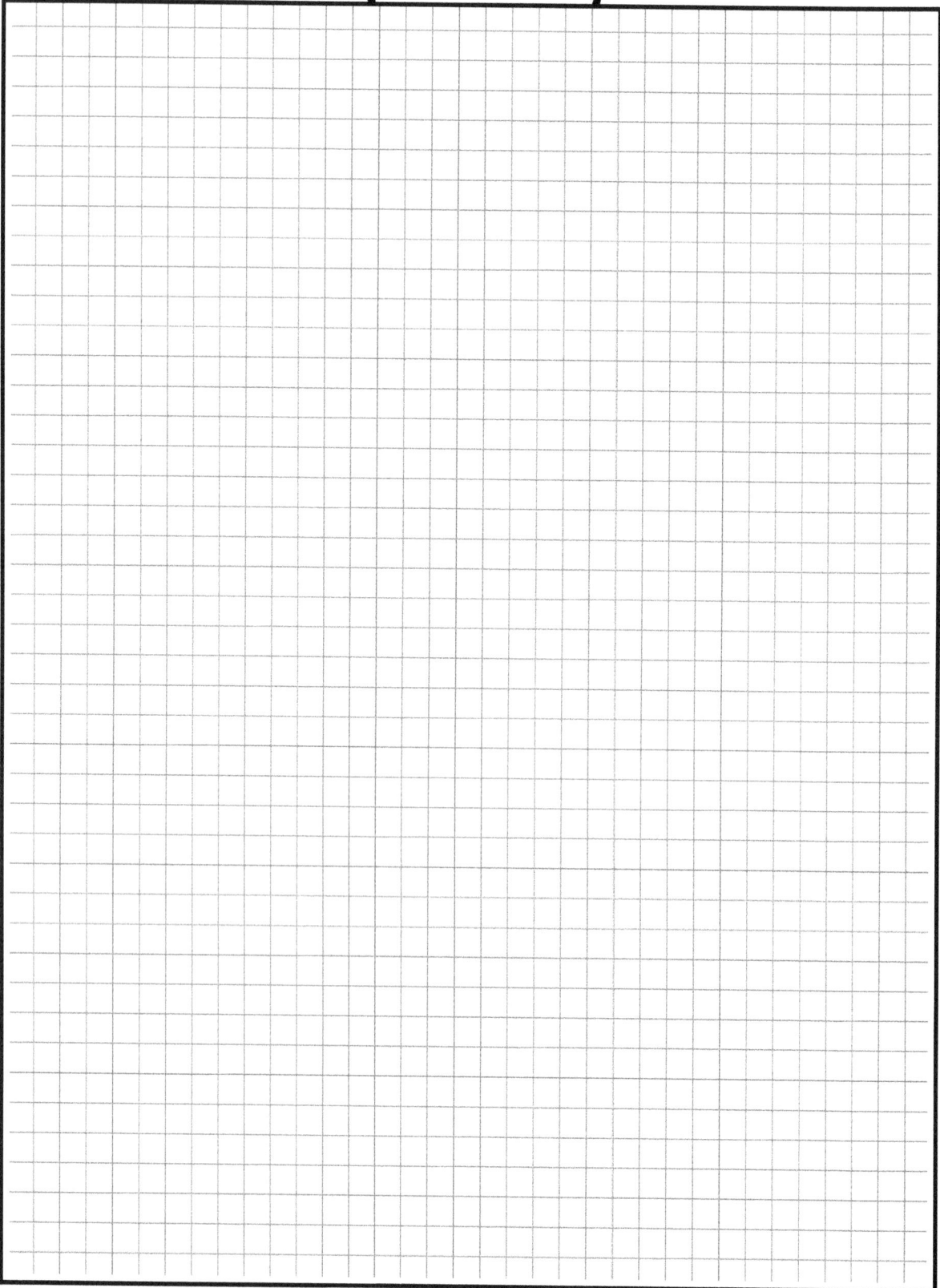

INVENTION

Description: _____

_____

_____

Designed / Created by: _____

Date created: _____

Where created: _____

Significance: _____

_____

_____

INVENTION NAME

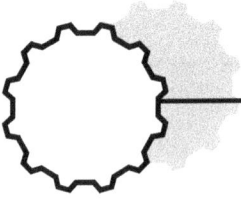

_____

- Function _____

_____

- How did you come up with the invention

_____

_____

- Importance of the Invention _____

_____

_____

Illustration of the Invention

FORMULAS & ROUGH SKETCHES

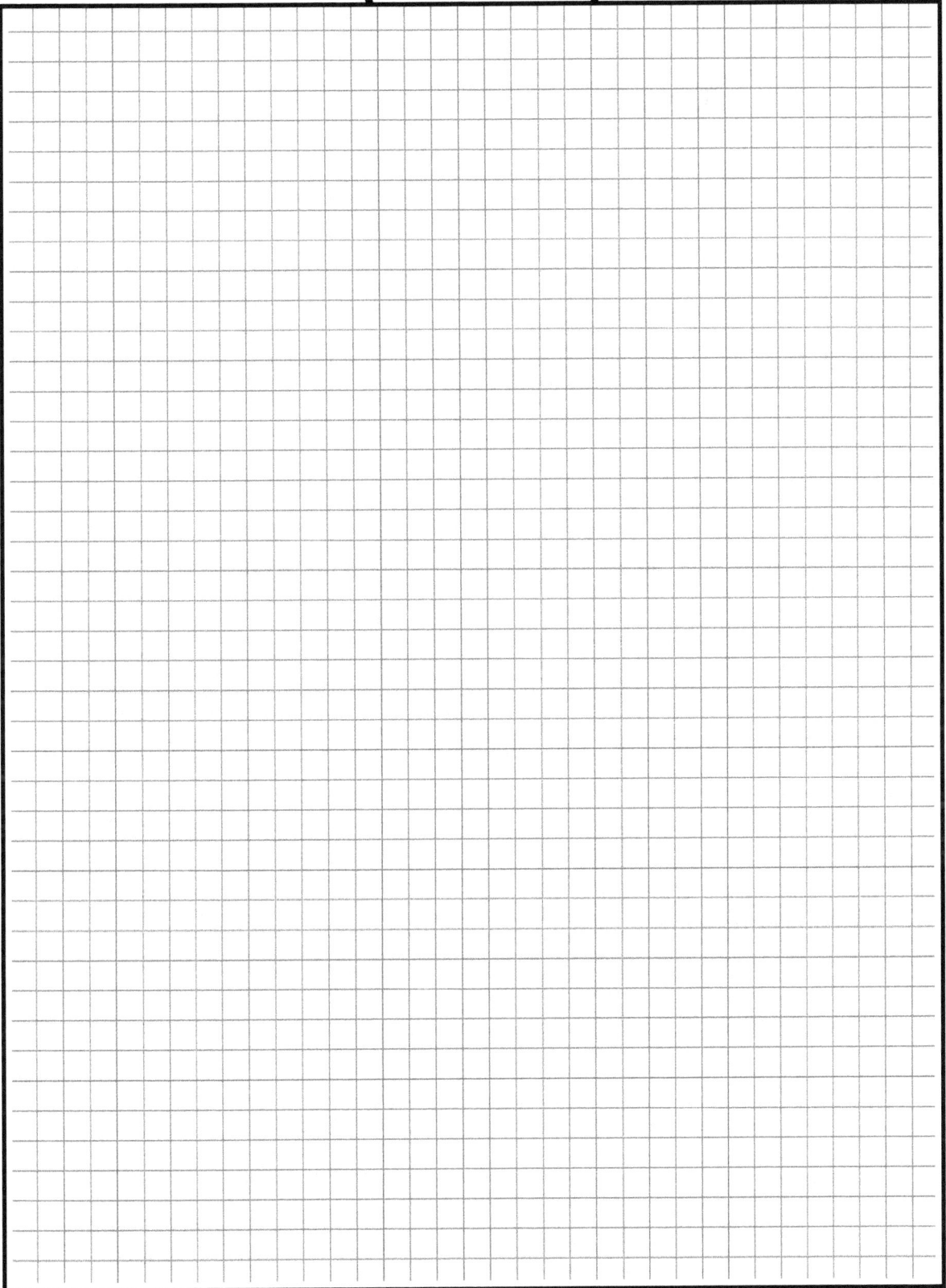

INVENTION

Description: _____
_____
_____

Designed / Created by: _____

Date created: _____

Where created: _____

Significance: _____
_____
_____

INVENTION NAME

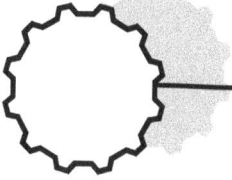

_____

- Function _____
_____

- How did you come up with the invention
_____
_____

- Importance of the Invention _____
_____
_____

Illustration of the Invention

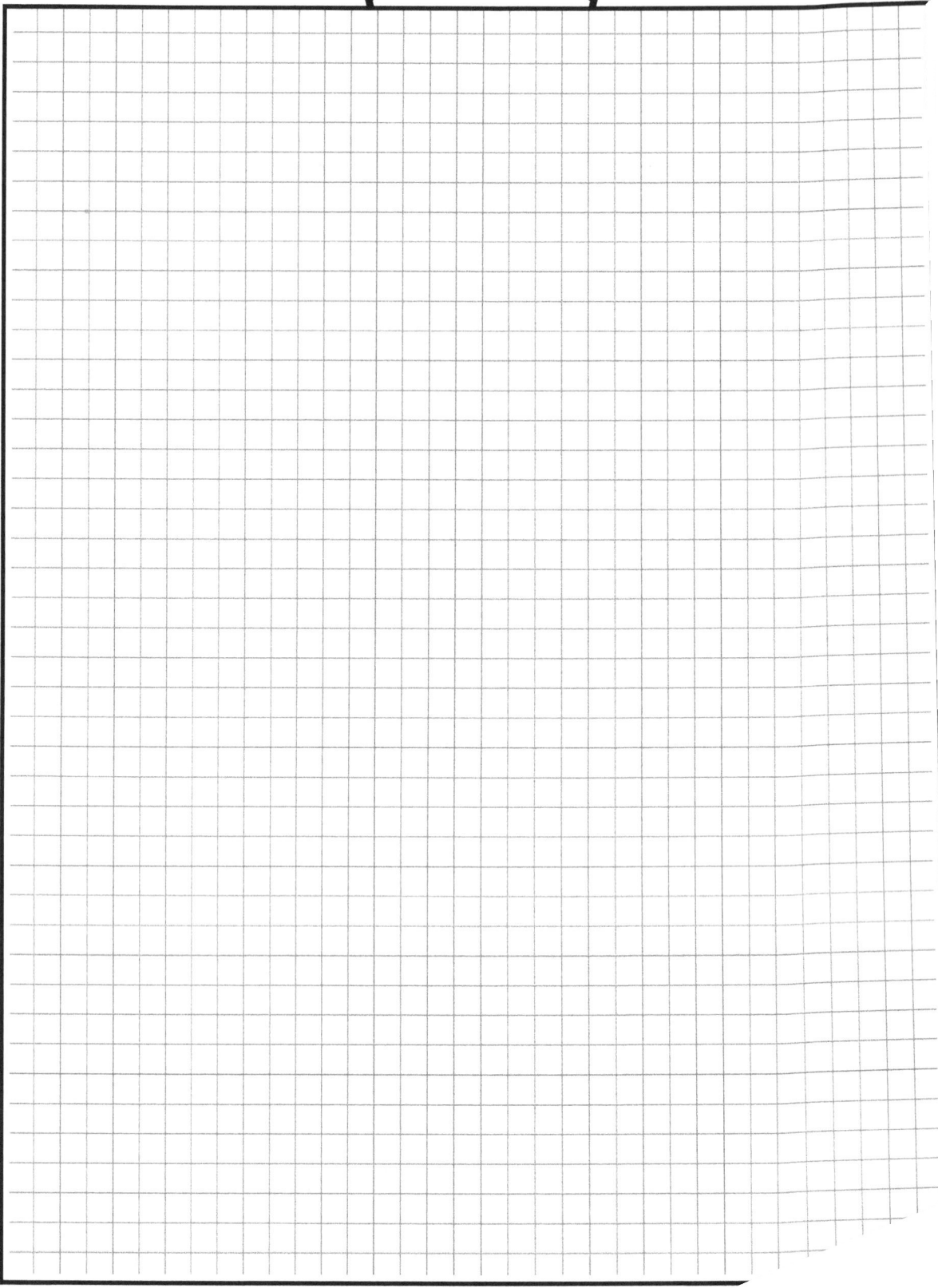

INVENTION

Description: _____

_____

_____

Designed / Created by: _____

Date created: _____

Where created: _____

Significance: _____

_____

_____

INVENTION NAME

• Function _____
_____

•   How did you come up with the invention
_____
_____

• Importance of the Invention _____
_____
_____

Illustration of the Invention

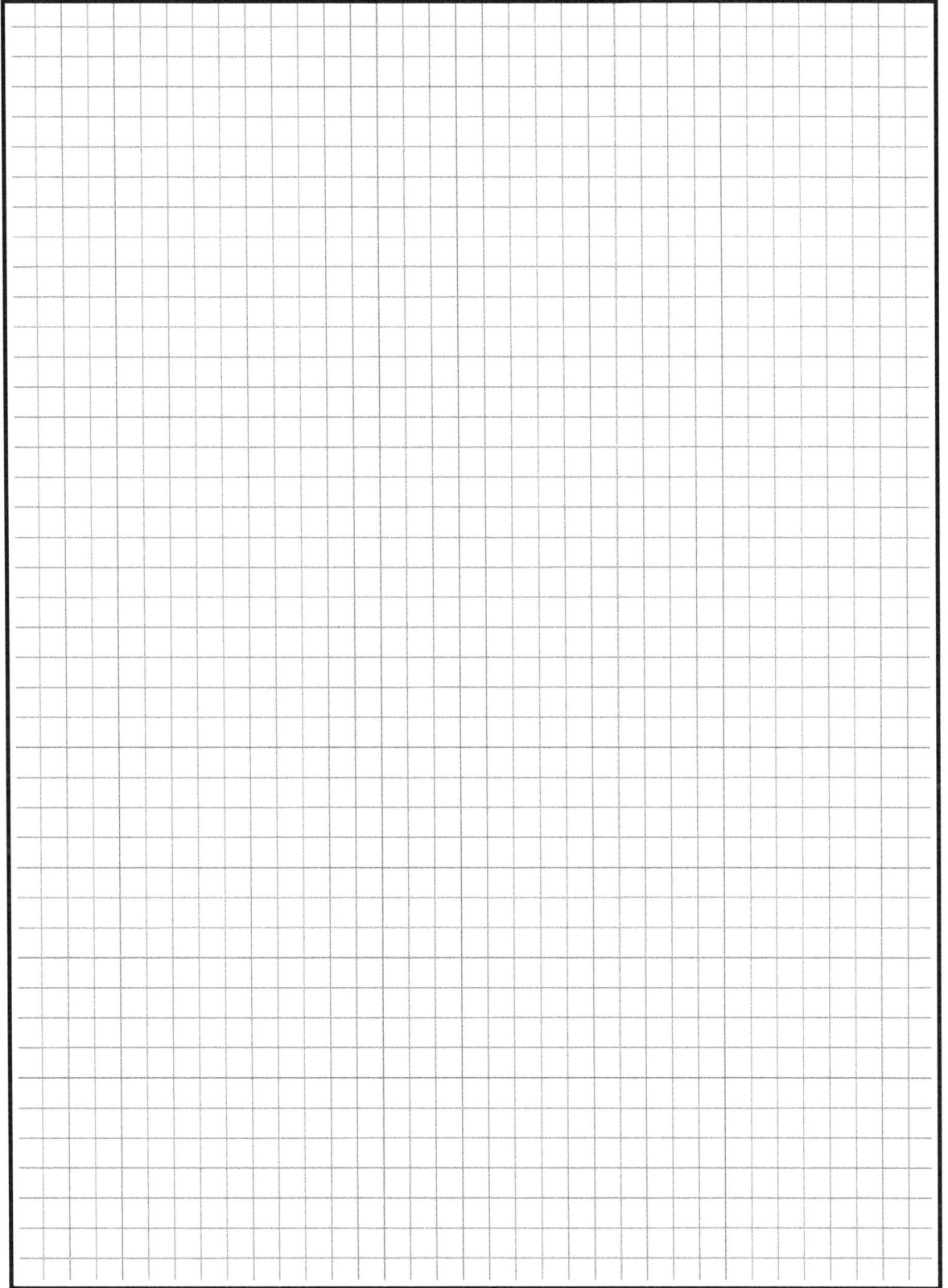

INVENTION

Description: _____

_____

_____

Designed / Created by: _____

Date created: _____

Where created: _____

Significance: _____

_____

_____

INVENTION NAME

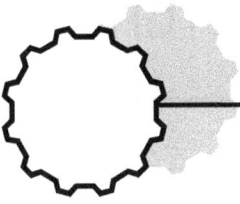

_____

• Function _____
_____

• How did you come up with the invention
_____
_____

• Importance of the Invention _____
_____
_____

Illustration of the Invention

FORMULAS & ROUGH SKETCHES

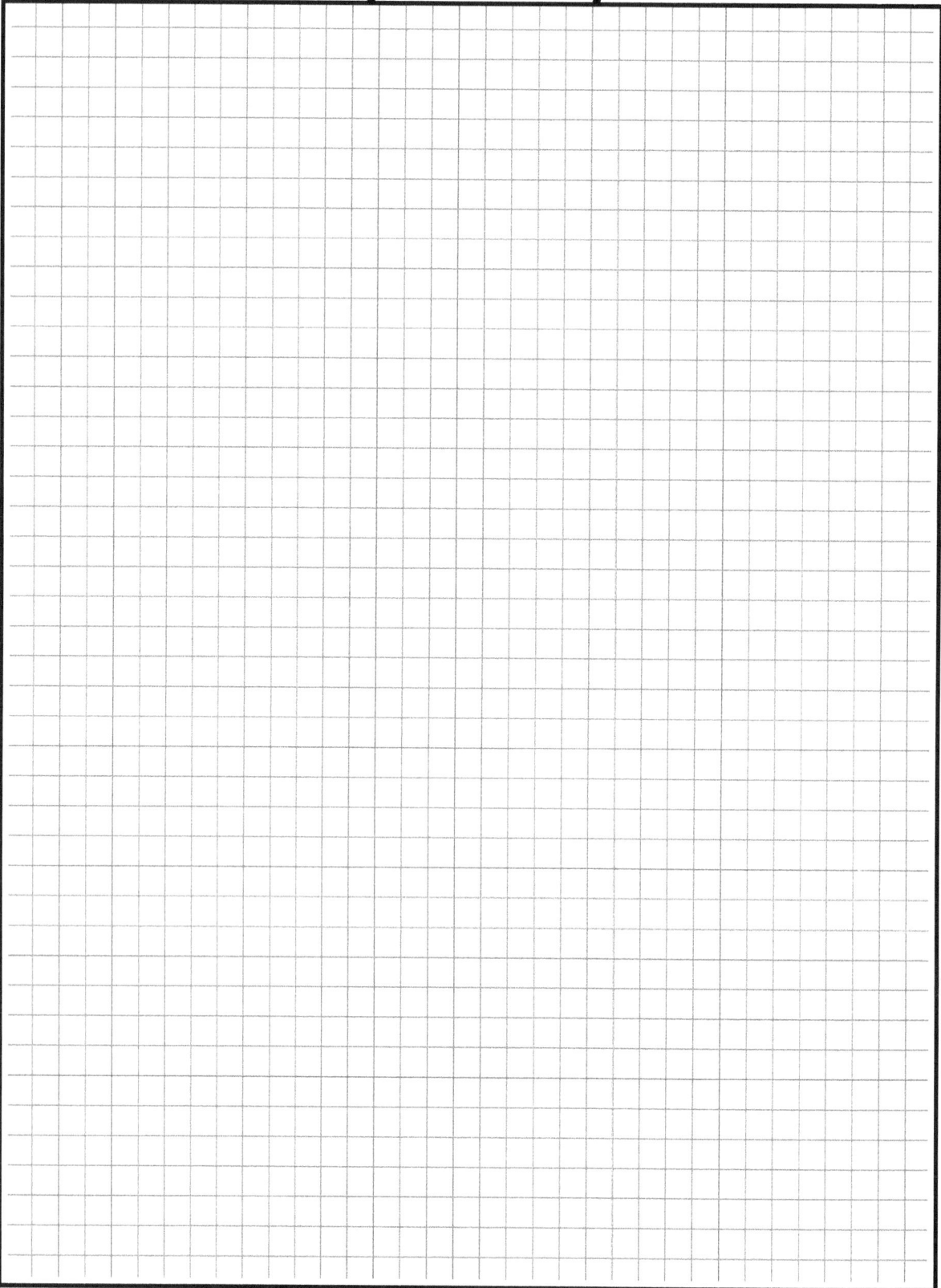

INVENTION

Description: _____

_____

_____

Designed / Created by: _____

Date created: _____

Where created: _____

Significance: _____

_____

_____

INVENTION NAME

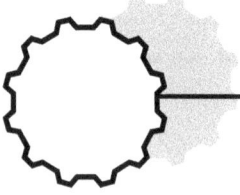

Function _____
_____

•   How did you come up with the invention
_____
_____

• Importance of the Invention _____
_____
_____

```
Illustration of the Invention
```

FORMULAS & ROUGH SKETCHES

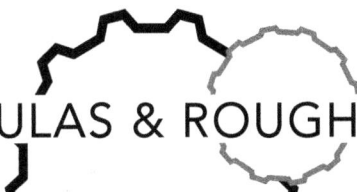

INVENTION

Description: _____

_____

_____

Designed / Created by: _____

Date created: _____

Where created: _____

Significance: _____

_____

_____

INVENTION NAME

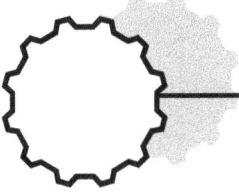

_____

- Function _____
_____

- How did you come up with the invention
_____
_____

- Importance of the Invention _____
_____
_____

Illustration of the Invention

FORMULAS & ROUGH SKETCHES

INVENTION

Description: _____
_____
_____

Designed / Created by: _____

Date created: _____

Where created: _____

Significance: _____
_____
_____

INVENTION NAME

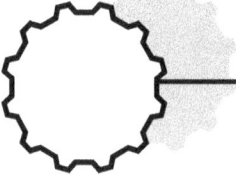

_____

- Function _____
_____

- How did you come up with the invention
_____
_____

- Importance of the Invention _____
_____
_____

Illustration of the Invention

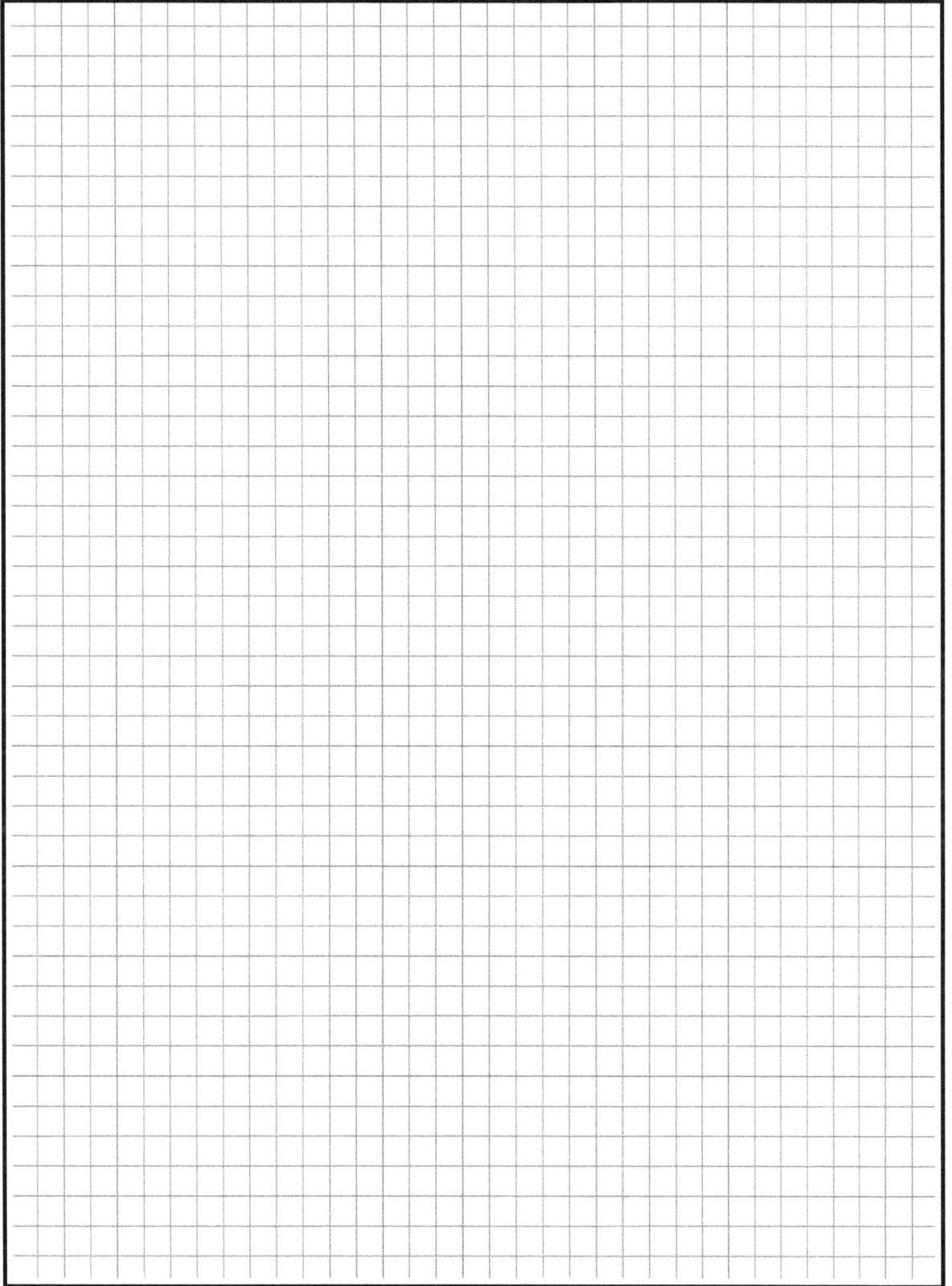

INVENTION

Description: _____
_____
_____

Designed / Created by: _____

Date created: _____

Where created: _____

Significance: _____
_____
_____

INVENTION NAME

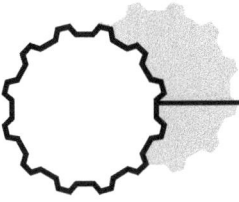

_____

- Function _____

_____

- How did you come up with the invention

_____

_____

- Importance of the Invention _____

_____

_____

Illustration of the Invention

FORMULAS & ROUGH SKETCHES

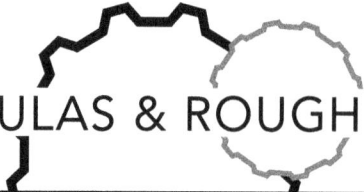

INVENTION

Description: _____
_____
_____

Designed / Created by: _____

Date created: _____

Where created: _____

Significance: _____
_____
_____

INVENTION NAME

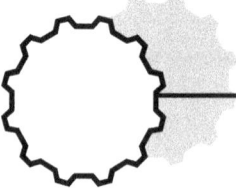

_____

- Function _____
_____

- How did you come up with the invention
_____
_____

- Importance of the Invention _____
_____
_____

Illustration of the Invention

FORMULAS & ROUGH SKETCHES

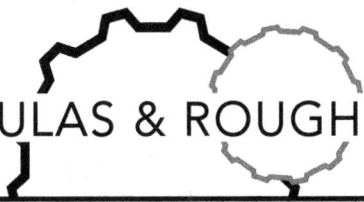

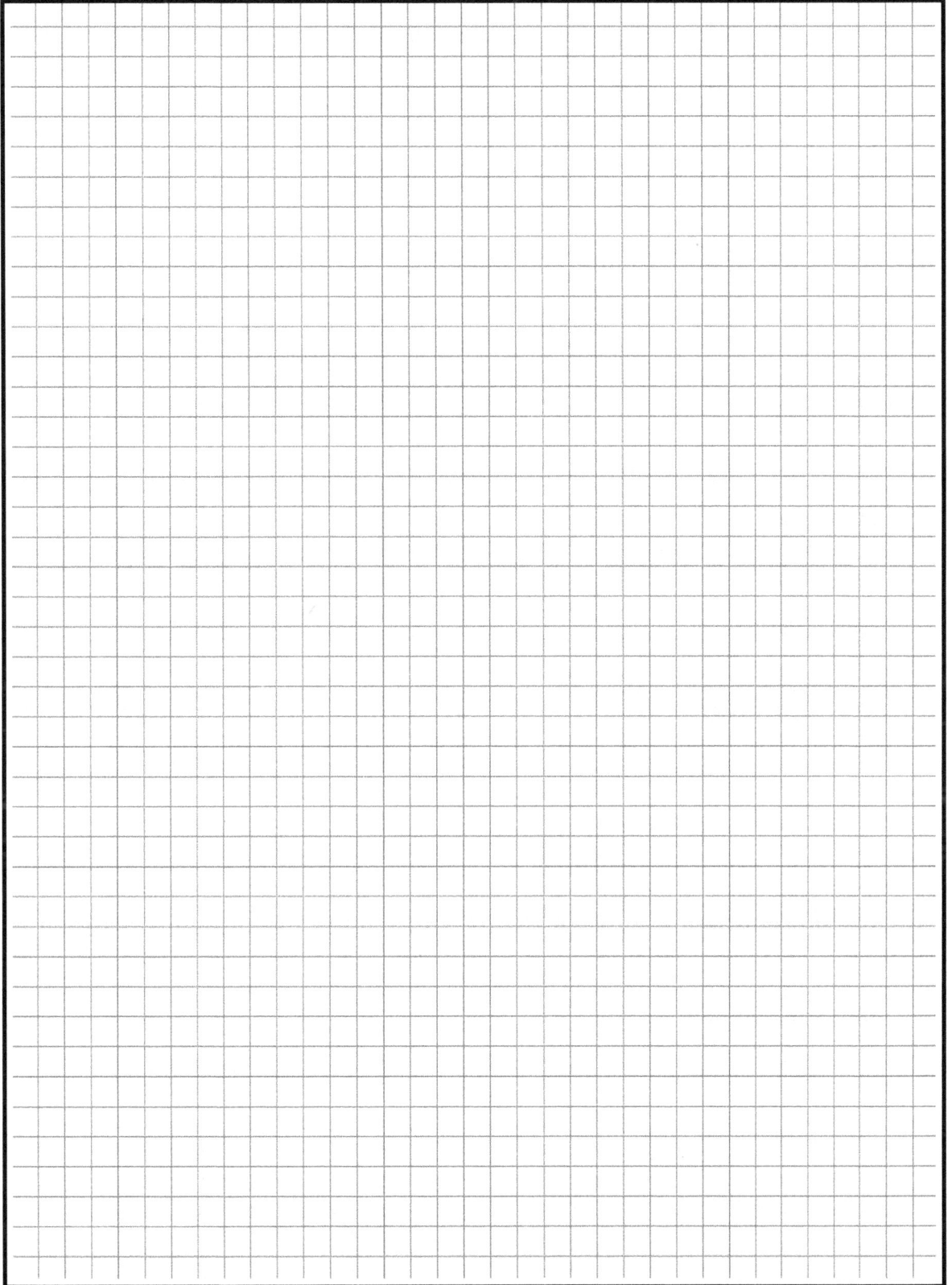

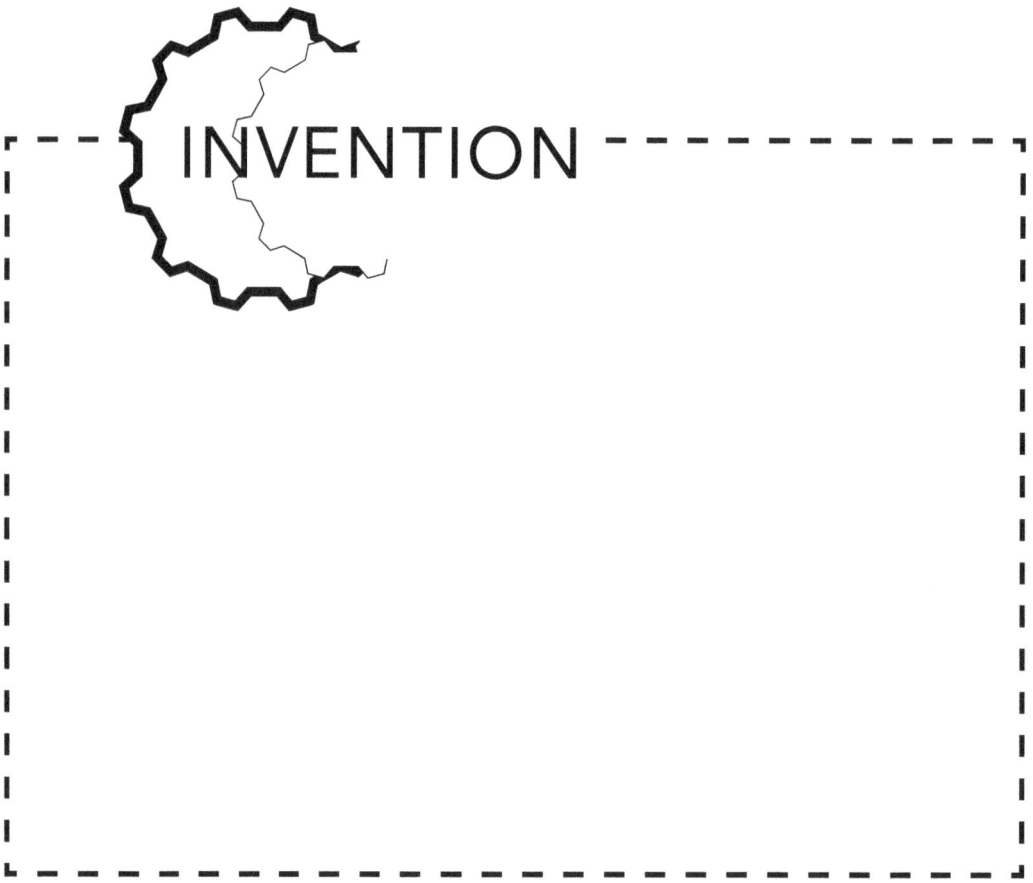

INVENTION

Description: _____

_____

_____

Designed / Created by: _____

Date created: _____

Where created: _____

Significance: _____

_____

_____

INVENTION NAME

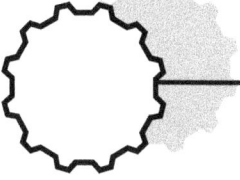

_____

- Function _____
_____

-    How did you come up with the invention
_____
_____

- Importance of the Invention _____
_____
_____

```
Illustration of the Invention




```

FORMULAS & ROUGH SKETCHES

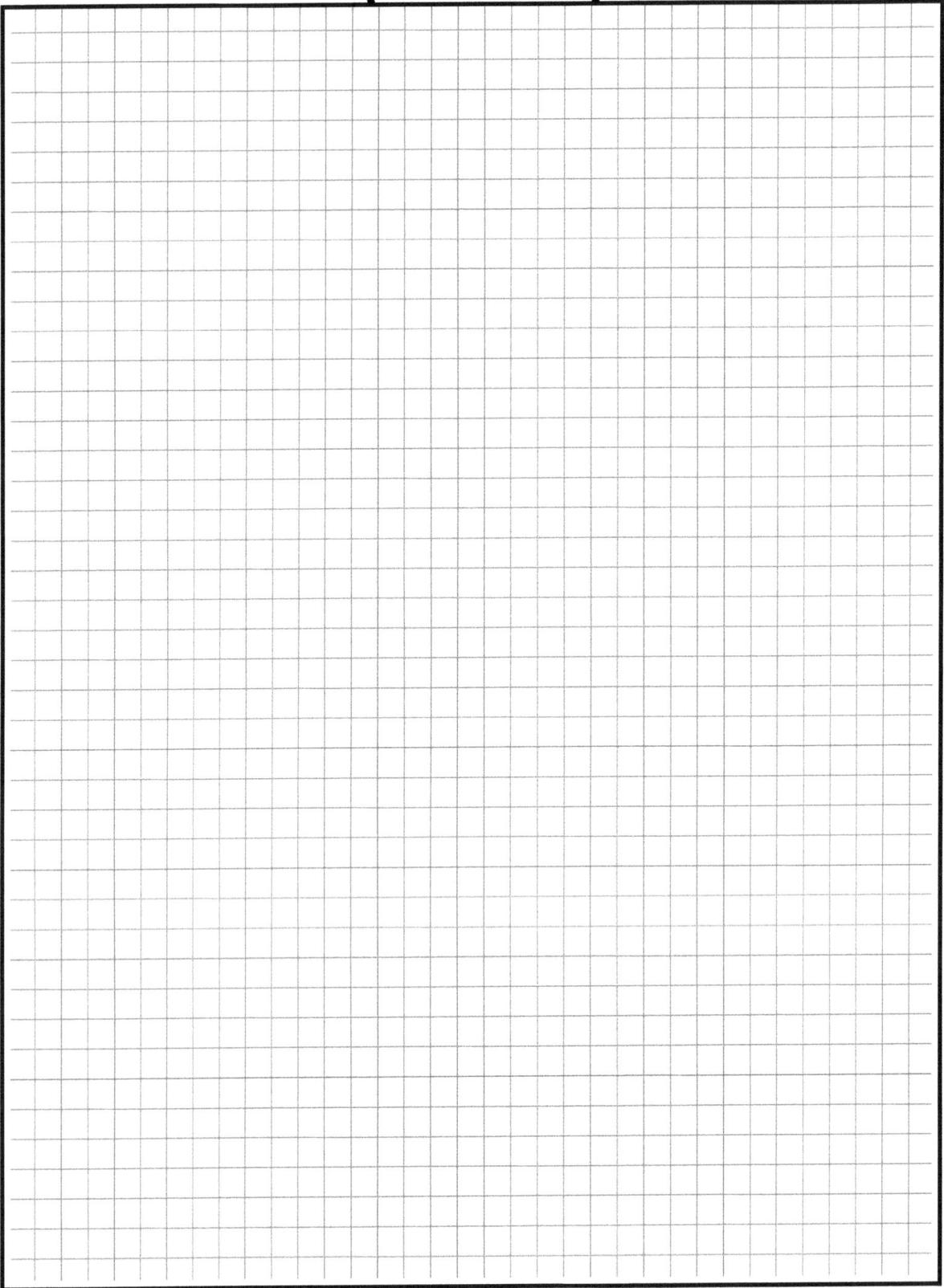

INVENTION

Description: _____

_____

_____

Designed / Created by: _____

Date created: _____

Where created: _____

Significance: _____

_____

_____

INVENTION NAME

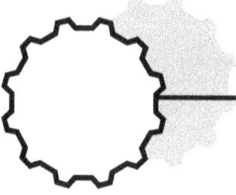

_____

• Function _____
_____

• How did you come up with the invention
_____
_____

• Importance of the Invention _____
_____
_____

Illustration of the Invention

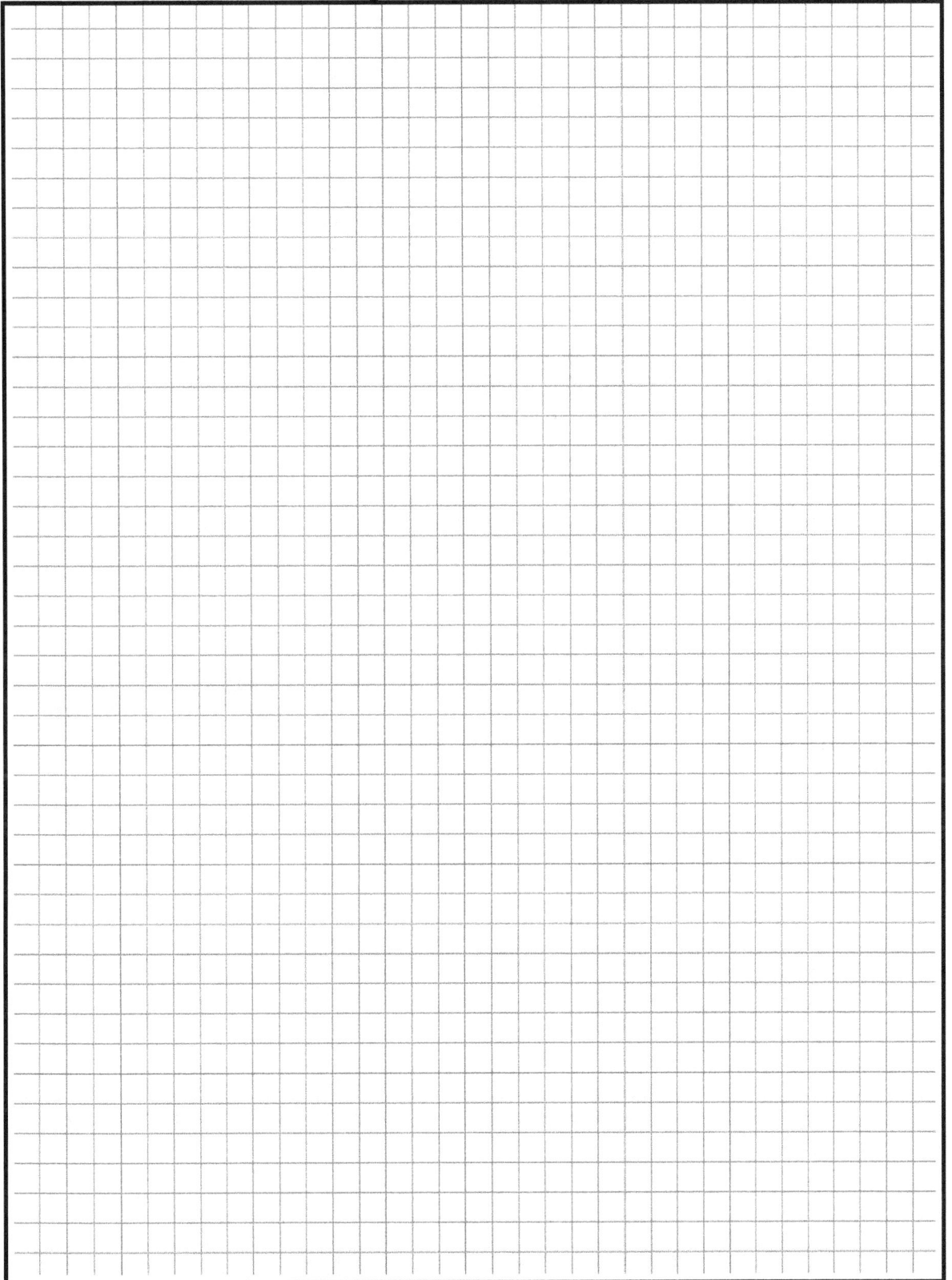

INVENTION

Description: _____
_____
_____

Designed / Created by: _____

Date created: _____

Where created: _____

Significance: _____
_____
_____

INVENTION NAME

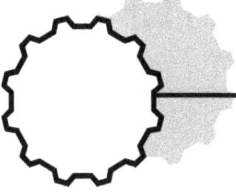

_____

- Function _____
_____

- How did you come up with the invention
_____
_____

- Importance of the Invention _____
_____
_____

Illustration of the Invention

FORMULAS & ROUGH SKETCHES

INVENTION

Description: _____
_____
_____

Designed / Created by: _____

Date created: _____

Where created: _____

Significance: _____
_____
_____

INVENTION NAME

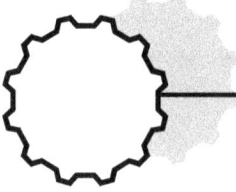

_____

- Function _____

_____

- How did you come up with the invention

_____

_____

- Importance of the Invention _____

_____

_____

```
Illustration of the Invention
```

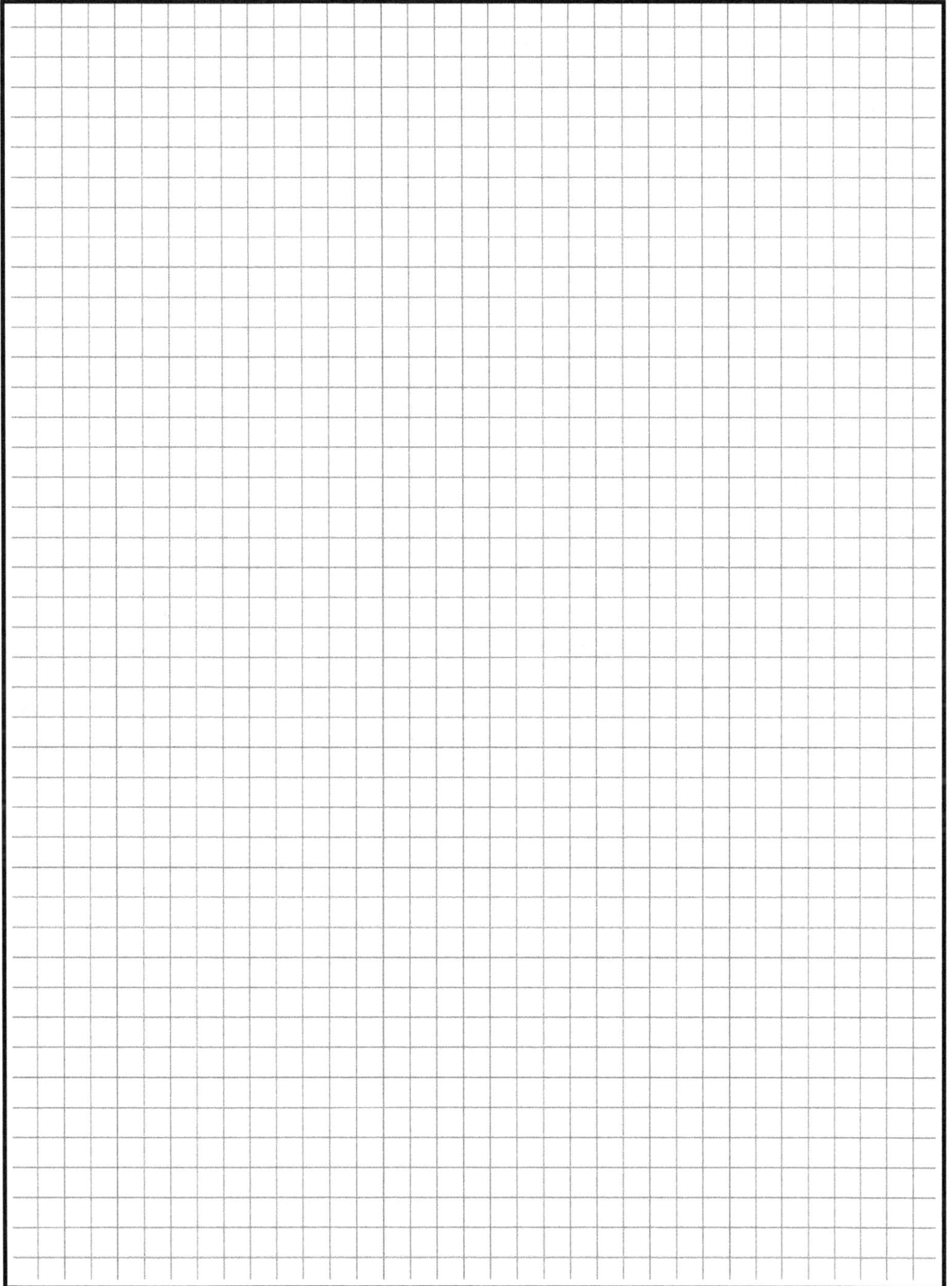

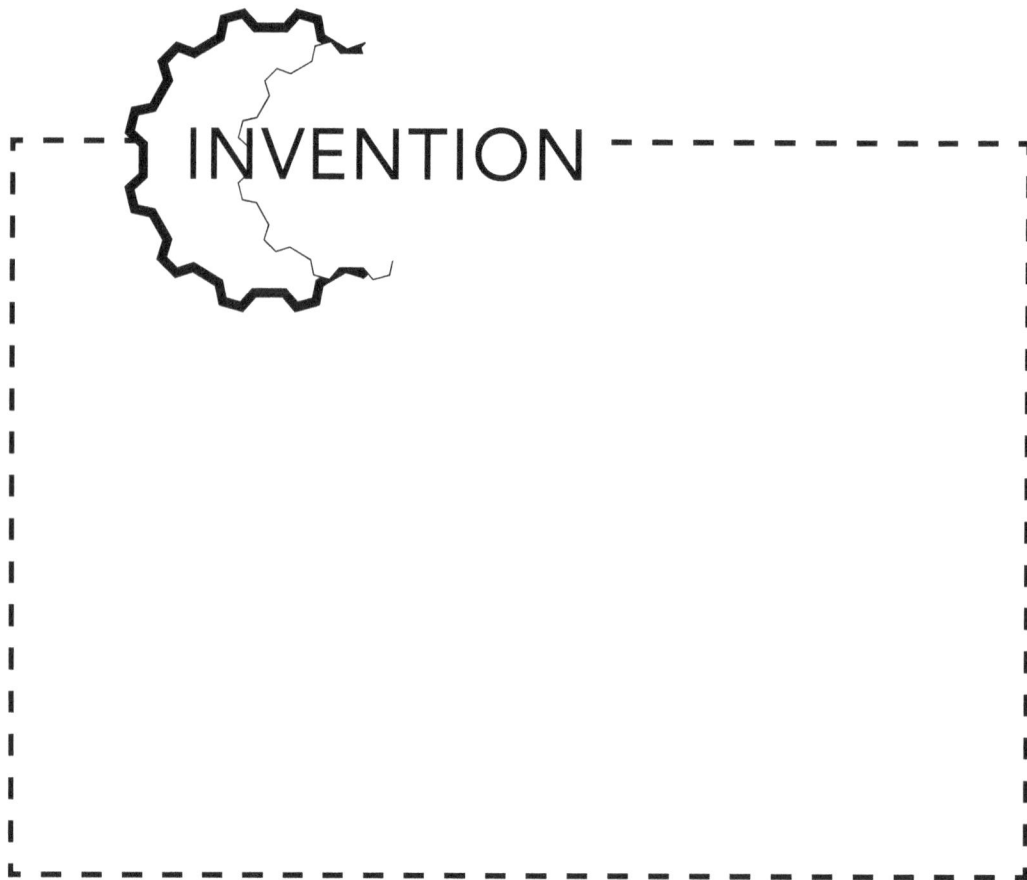

INVENTION

Description: _____
_____
_____

Designed / Created by: _____

Date created: _____

Where created: _____

Significance: _____
_____
_____

INVENTION NAME

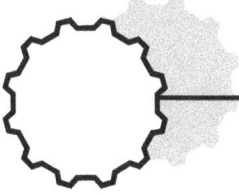

_____

- Function _____
_____

- How did you come up with the invention
_____
_____

- Importance of the Invention _____
_____
_____

Illustration of the Invention

INVENTION

Description: _____

_____

_____

Designed / Created by: _____

Date created: _____

Where created: _____

Significance: _____

_____

_____

INVENTION NAME

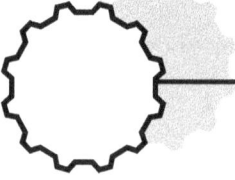

_____

- Function _____
_____

- How did you come up with the invention
_____
_____

- Importance of the Invention _____
_____
_____

Illustration of the Invention

FORMULAS & ROUGH SKETCHES

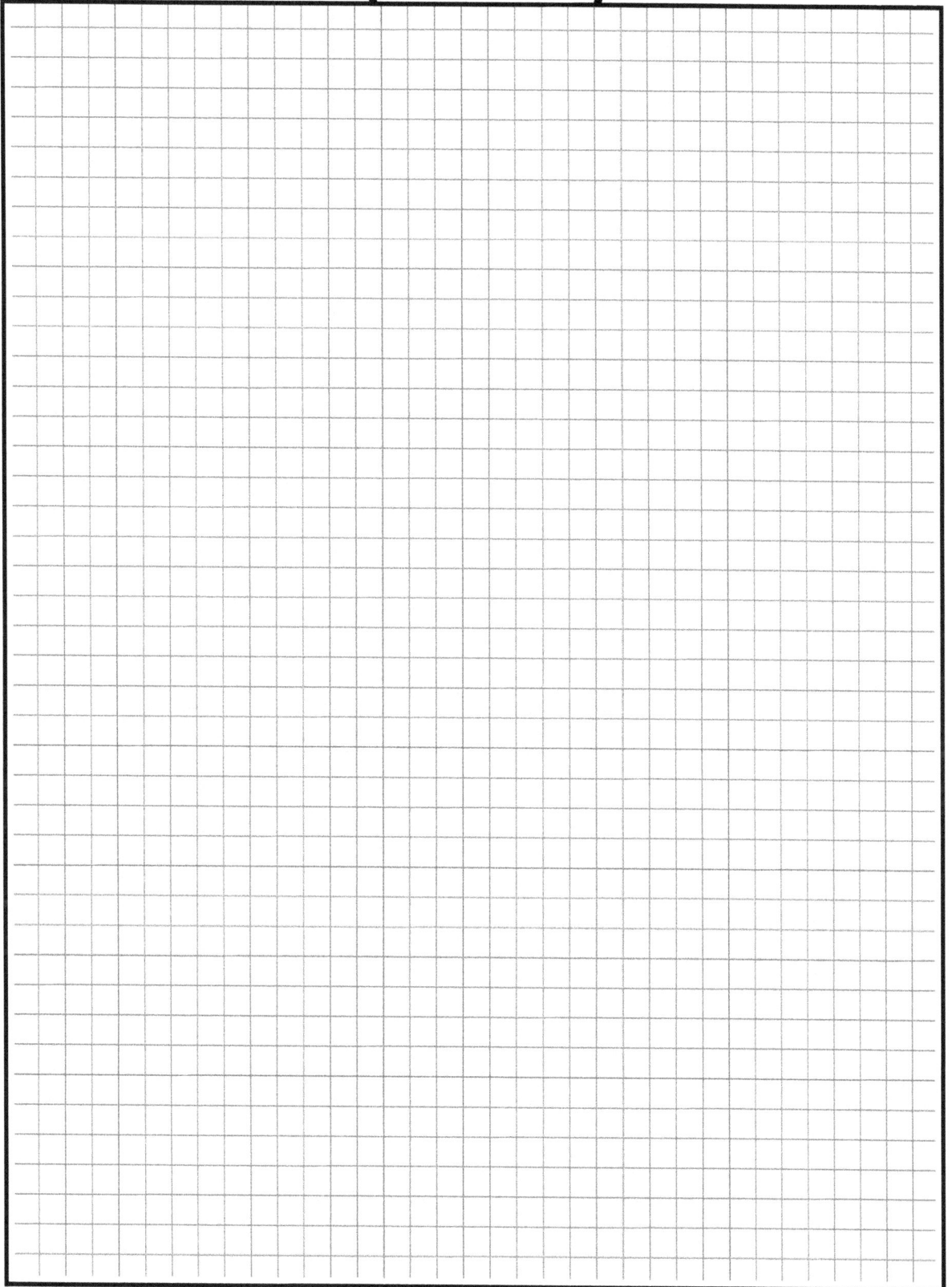

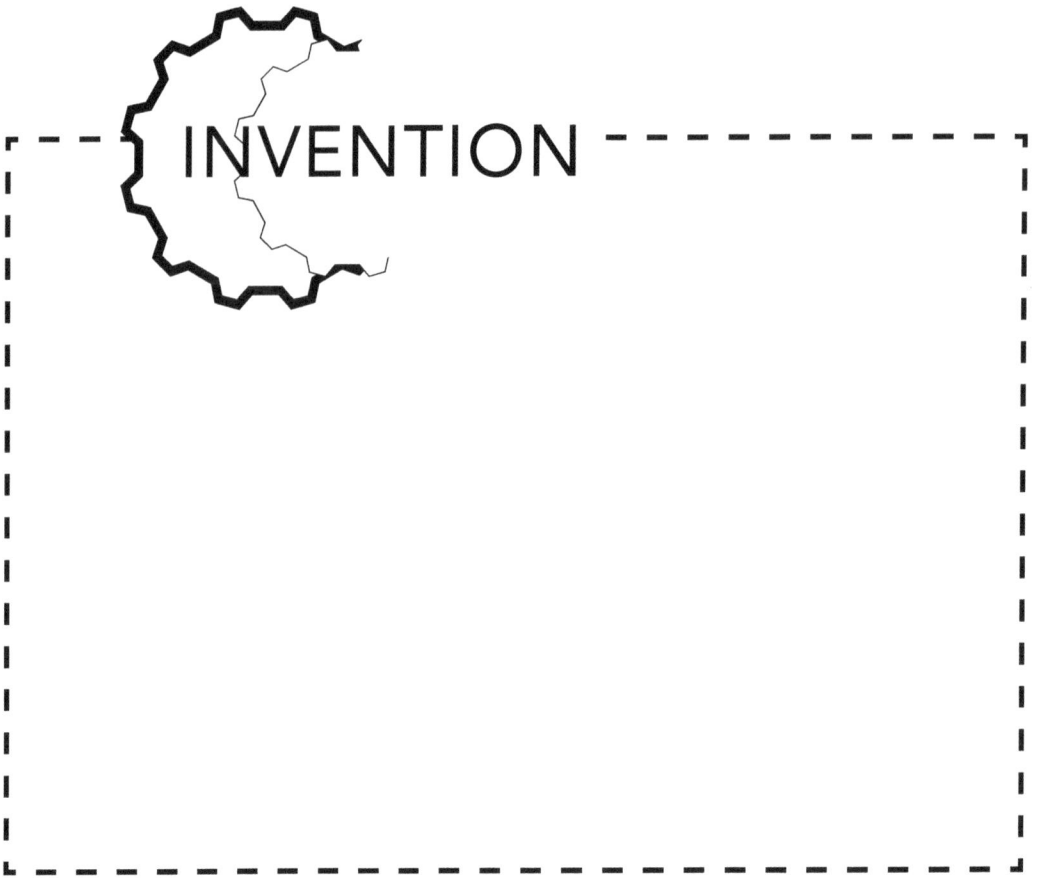

INVENTION

Description: _____
_____
_____

Designed / Created by: _____

Date created: _____

Where created: _____

Significance: _____
_____
_____

INVENTION NAME

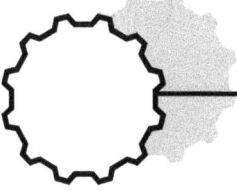

_____

- Function _____
_____

- How did you come up with the invention
_____
_____

- Importance of the Invention _____
_____
_____

Illustration of the Invention

FORMULAS & ROUGH SKETCHES

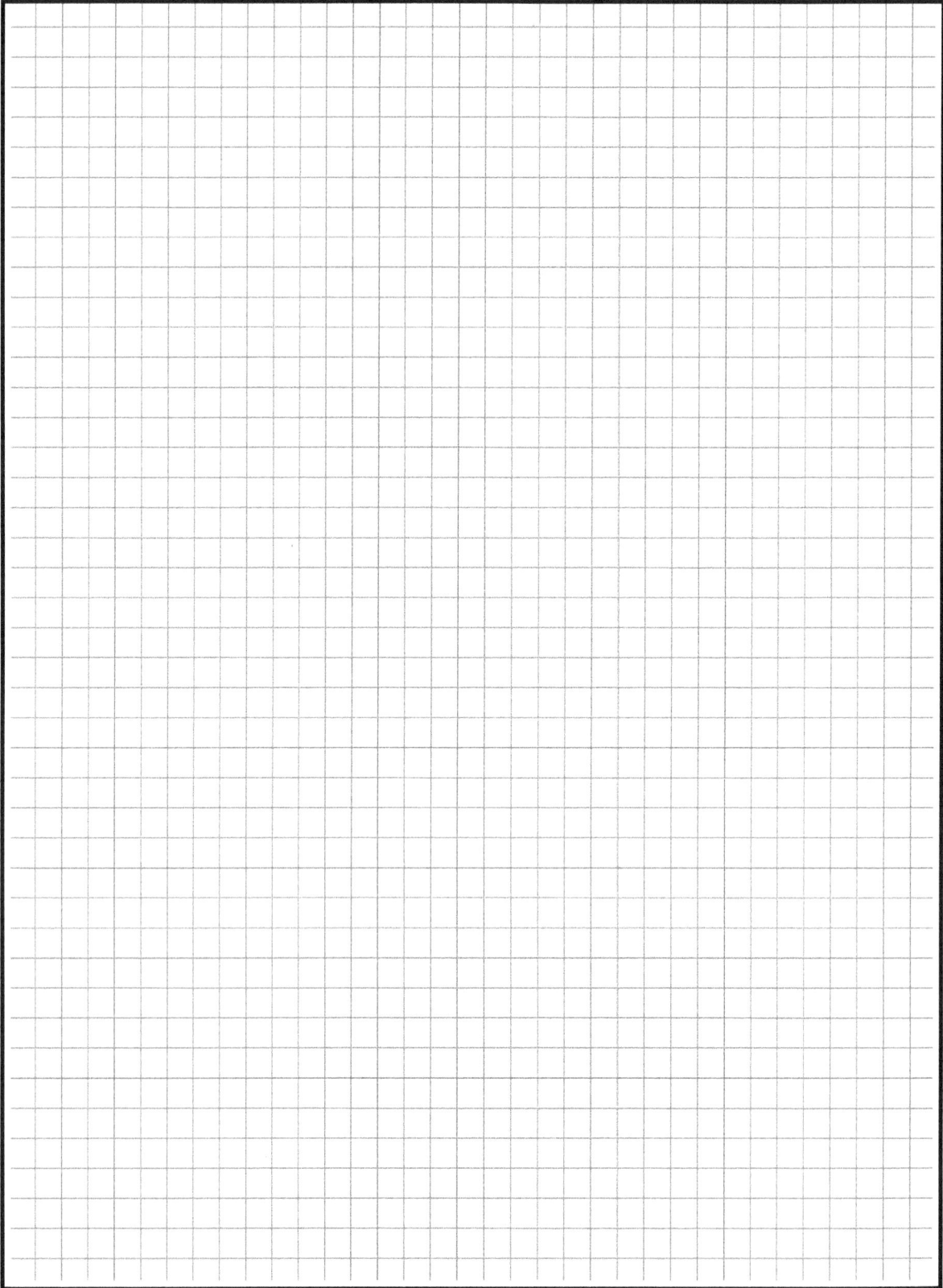

INVENTION

Description: _____

_____

_____

Designed / Created by: _____

Date created: _____

Where created: _____

Significance: _____

_____

_____

INVENTION NAME

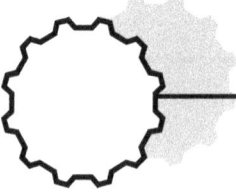

_____

• Function _____
_____

• How did you come up with the invention
_____
_____

• Importance of the Invention _____
_____
_____

Illustration of the Invention

FORMULAS & ROUGH SKETCHES

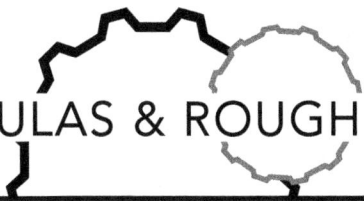

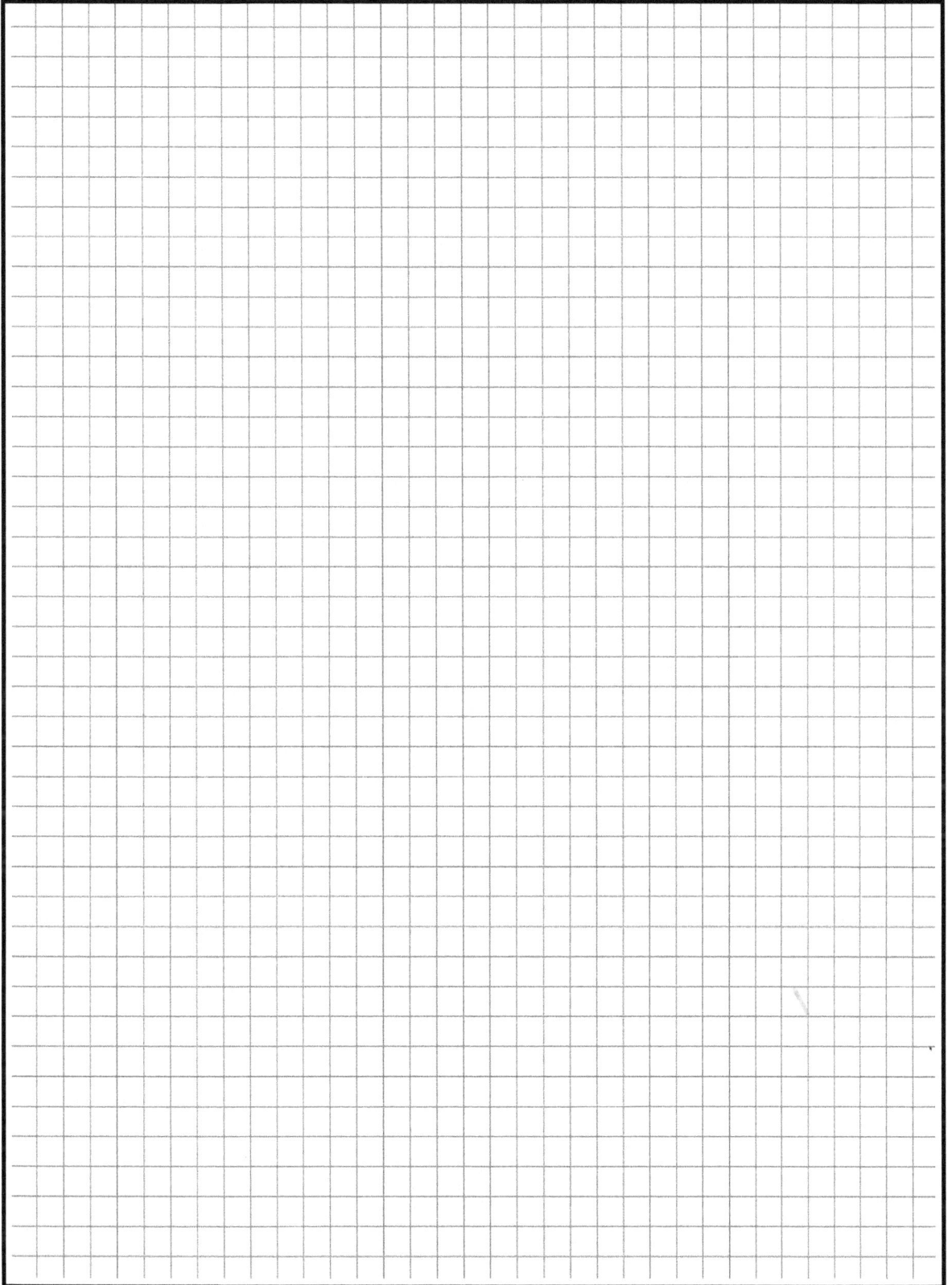

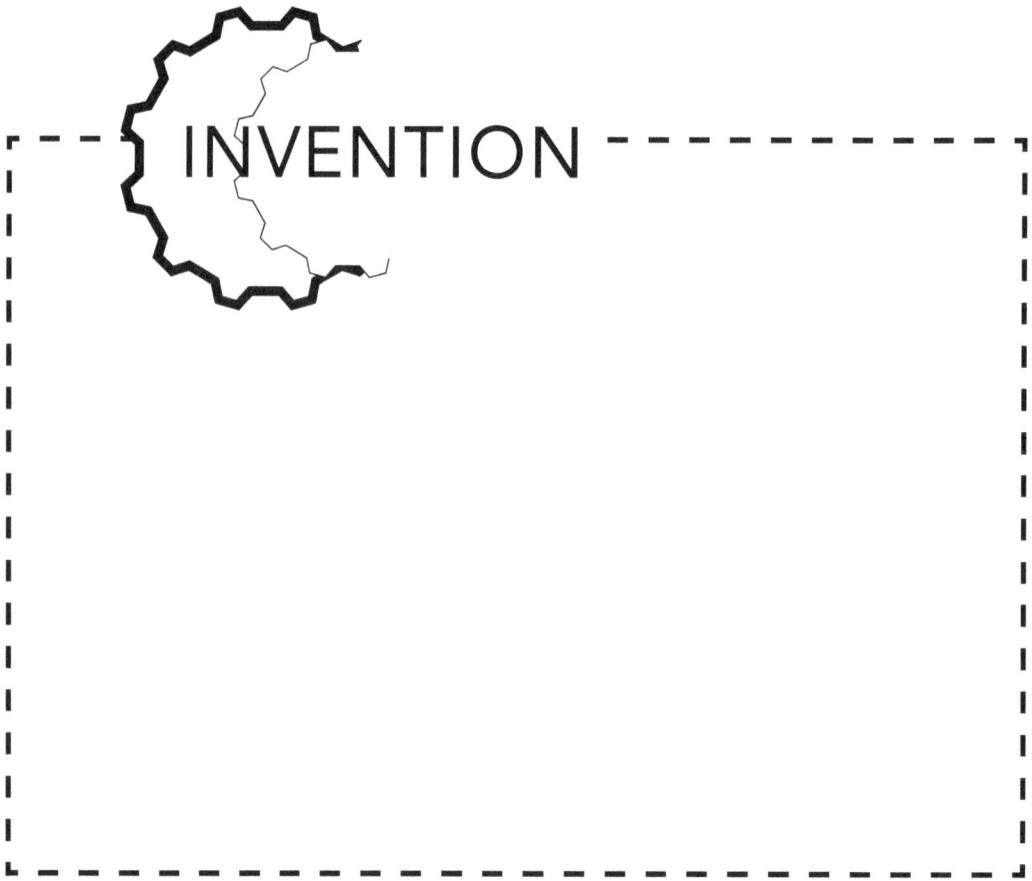

INVENTION

Description: _____

_____

_____

Designed / Created by: _____

Date created: _____

Where created: _____

Significance: _____

_____

_____

INVENTION NAME

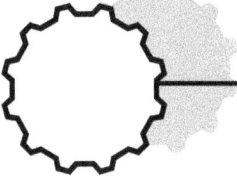

_____

• Function _____
_____

• How did you come up with the invention
_____
_____

• Importance of the Invention _____
_____
_____

Illustration of the Invention

FORMULAS & ROUGH SKETCHES

INVENTION

Description: _____

_____

_____

Designed / Created by: _____

Date created: _____

Where created: _____

Significance: _____

_____

_____

INVENTION NAME

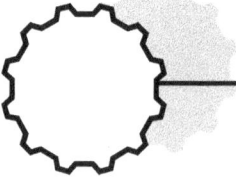

⊙ _____

• Function _____
_____

•   How did you come up with the invention
_____
_____

• Importance of the Invention _____
_____
_____

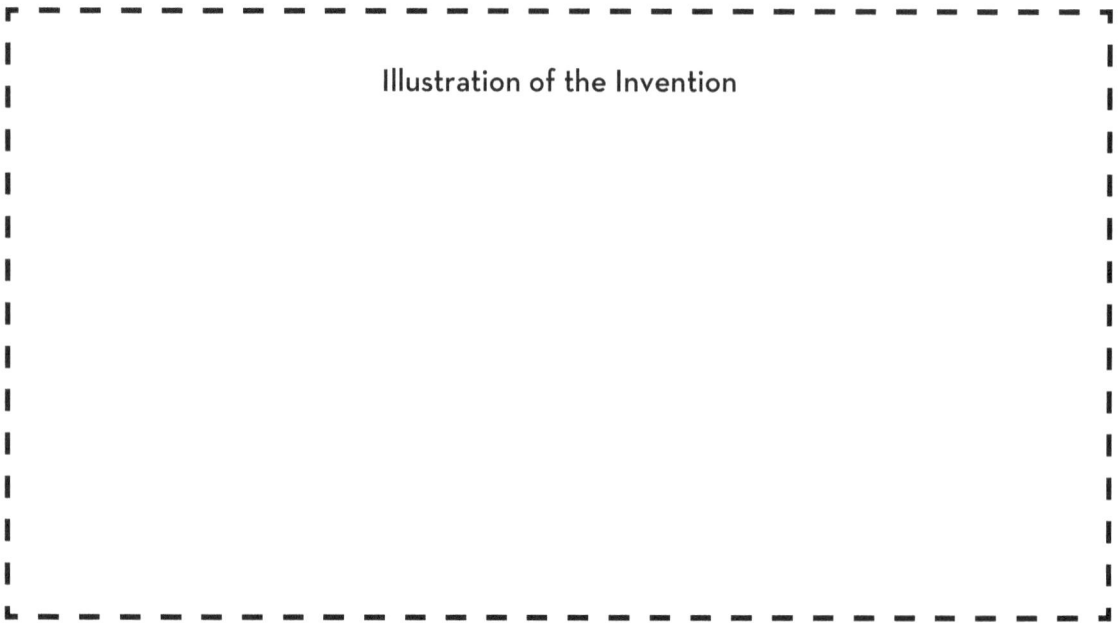

Illustration of the Invention

FORMULAS & ROUGH SKETCHES

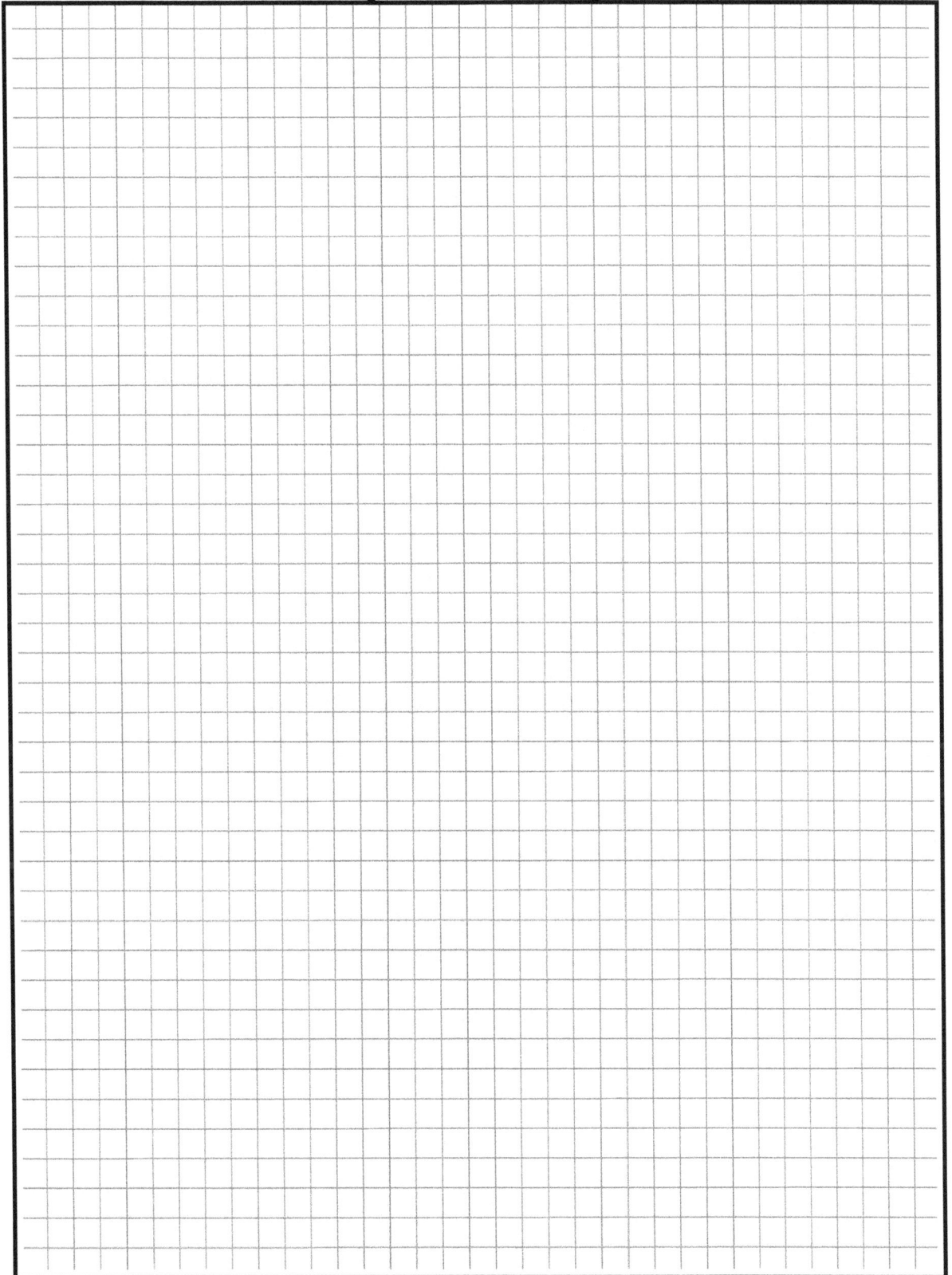

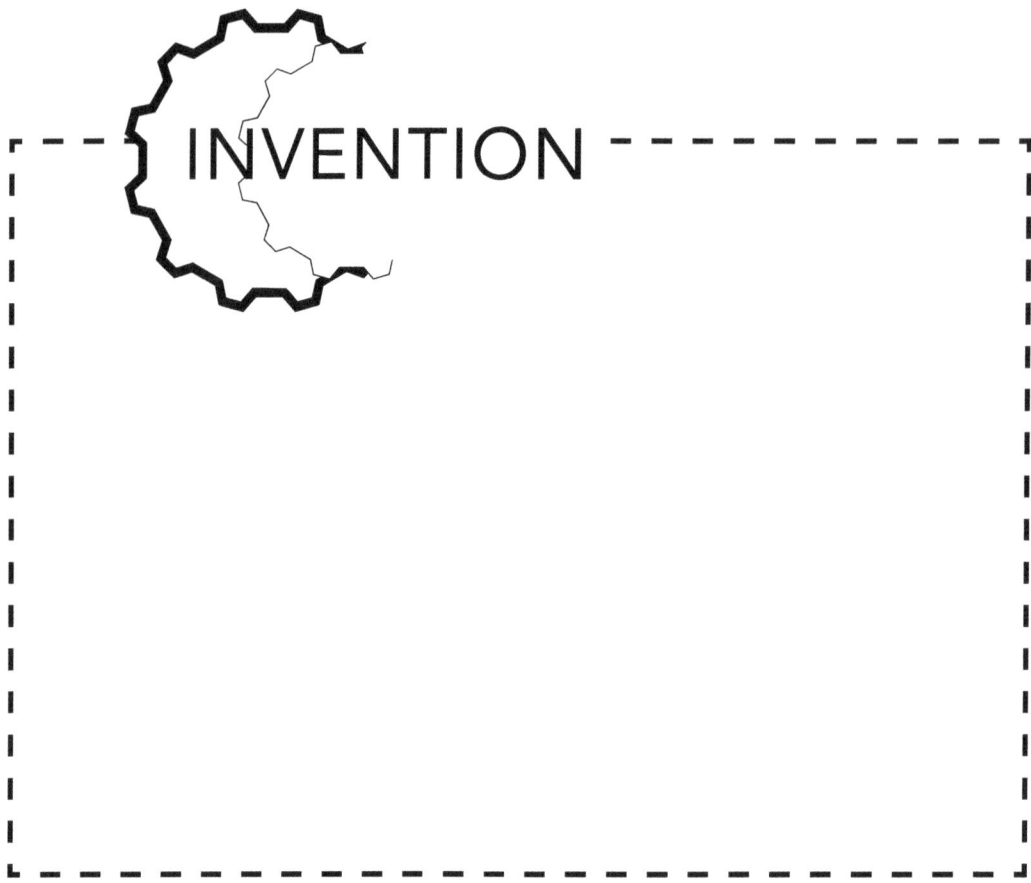

INVENTION

Description: _____

_____

_____

Designed / Created by: _____

Date created: _____

Where created: _____

Significance: _____

_____

_____

INVENTION NAME

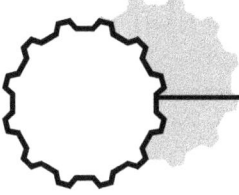

_____

- Function _____
_____

- How did you come up with the invention
_____
_____

- Importance of the Invention _____
_____
_____

Illustration of the Invention

FORMULAS & ROUGH SKETCHES

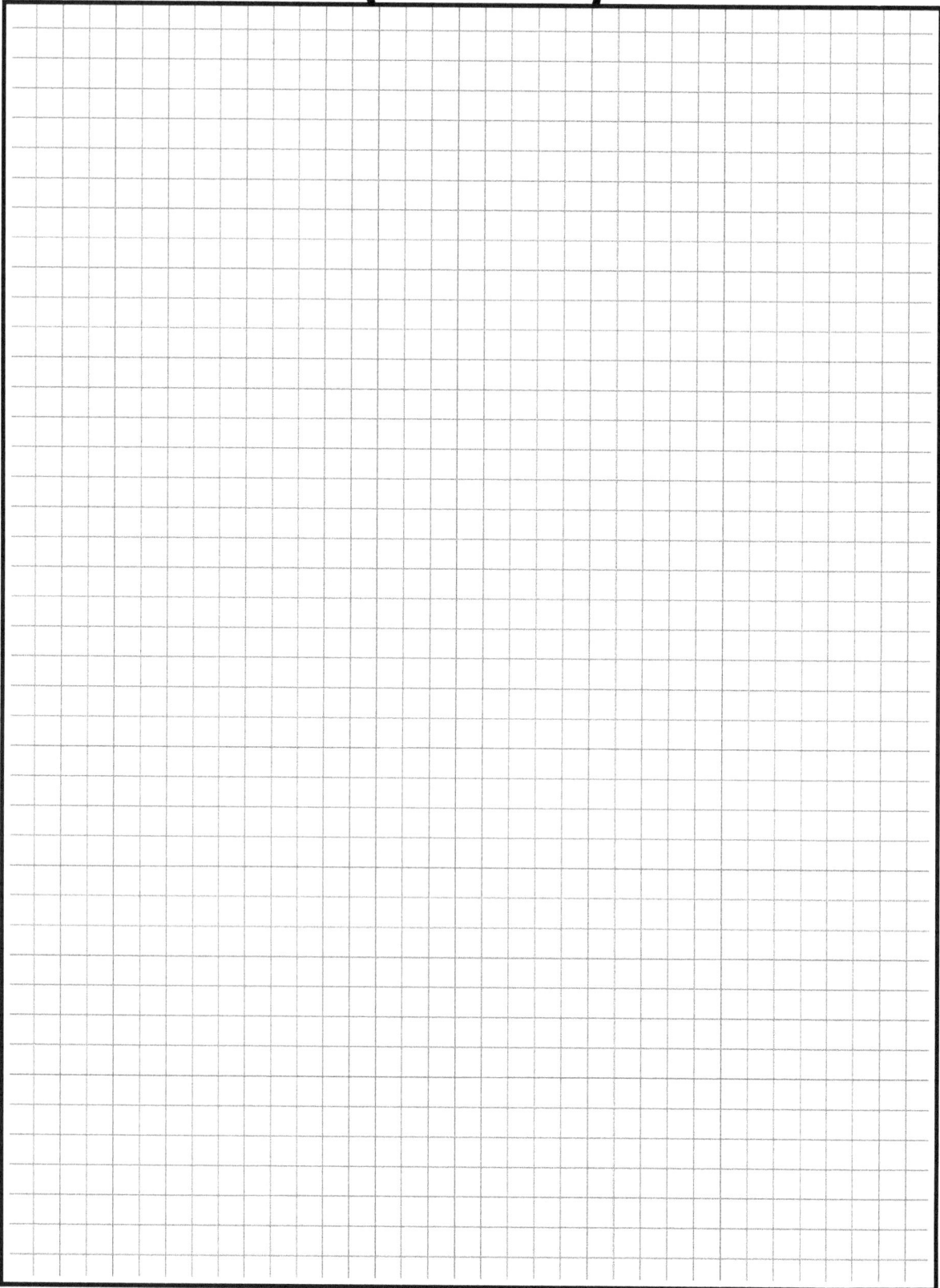

INVENTION

Description: _____

_____

_____

Designed / Created by: _____

Date created: _____

Where created: _____

Significance: _____

_____

_____

INVENTION NAME

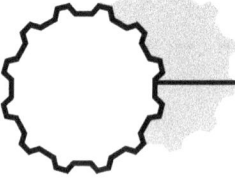

_____

- Function _____
_____

- How did you come up with the invention
_____
_____

- Importance of the Invention _____
_____
_____

Illustration of the Invention

FORMULAS & ROUGH SKETCHES

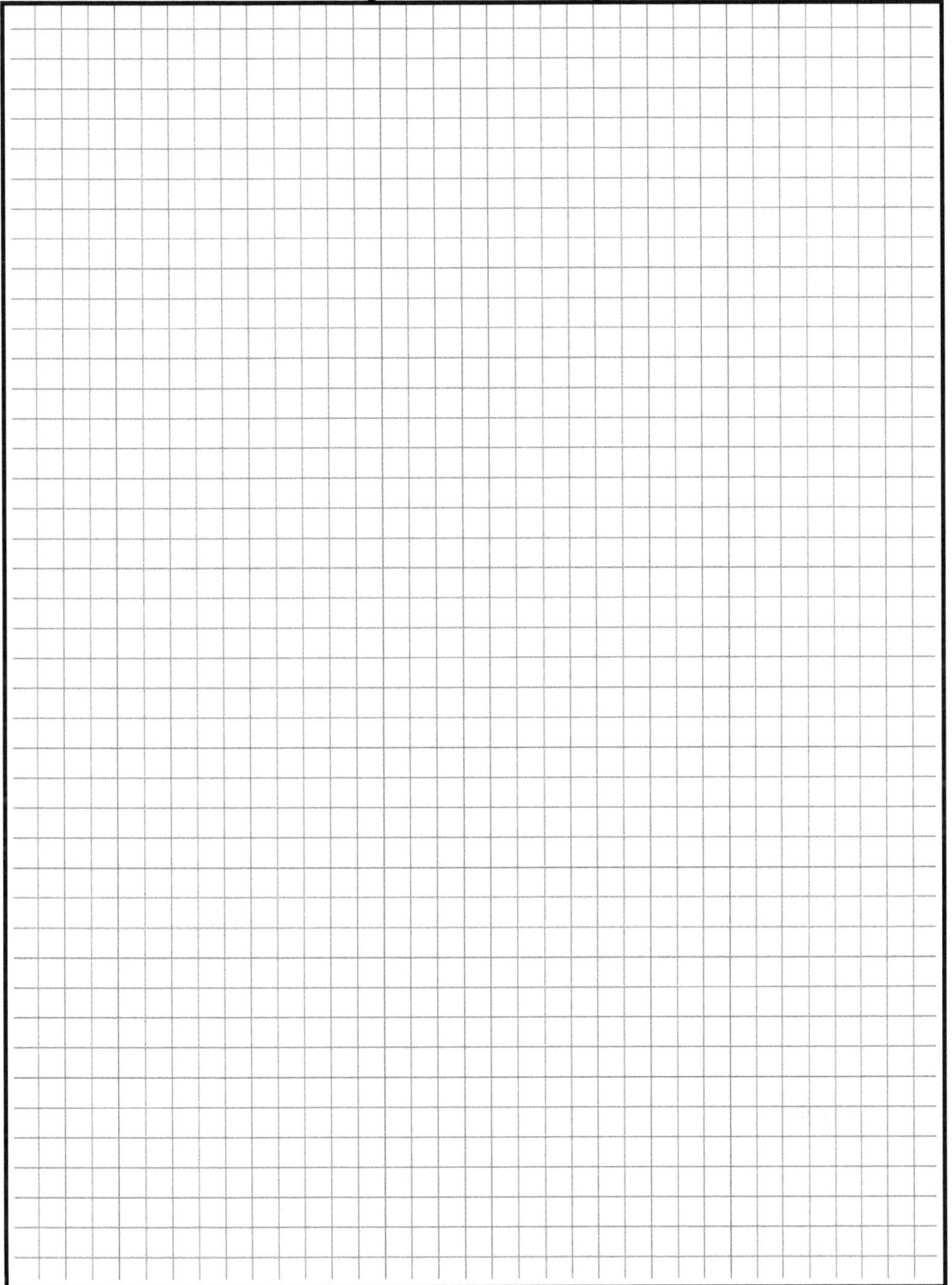

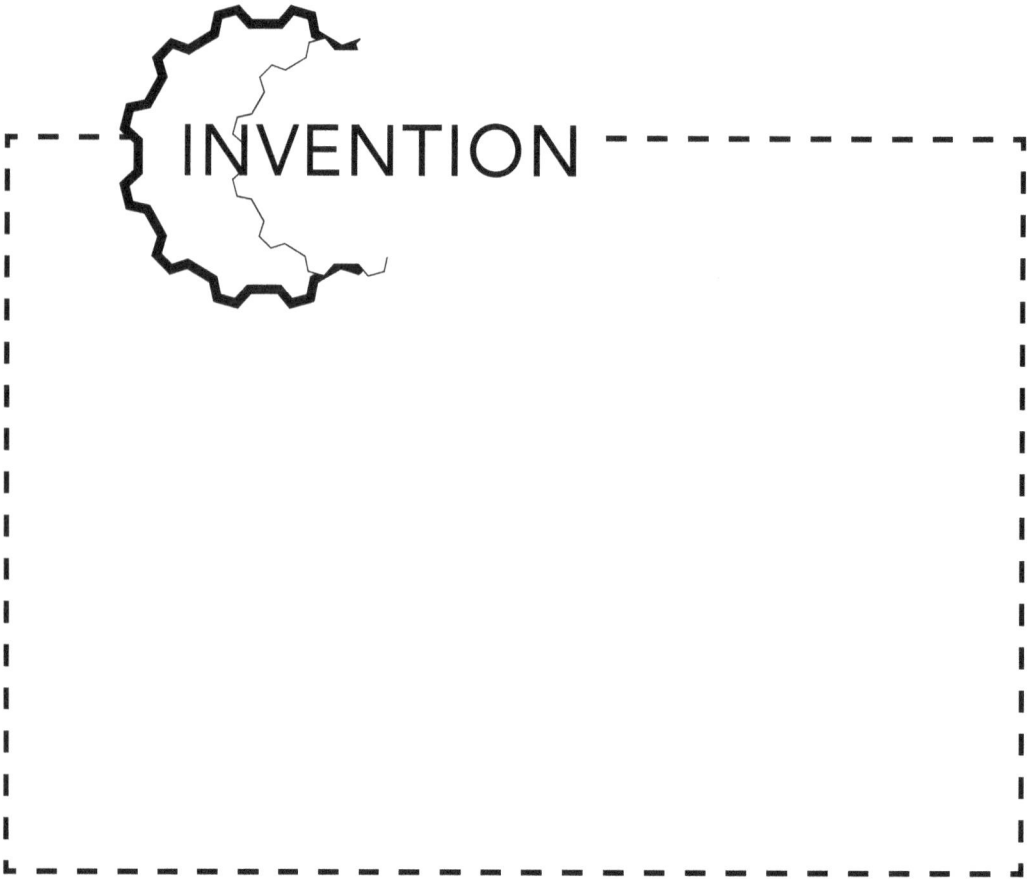

INVENTION

Description: _____
_____
_____

Designed / Created by: _____

Date created: _____

Where created: _____

Significance: _____
_____
_____

INVENTION NAME

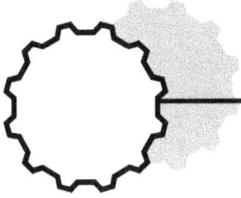

_____

- Function _____
_____

- How did you come up with the invention
_____
_____

- Importance of the Invention _____
_____
_____

```
┌ ─ ─ ─ ─ ─ ─ ─ ─ ─ ─ ─ ─ ─ ─ ─ ┐
│           Illustration of the Invention           │
│                                               │
│                                               │
│                                               │
│                                               │
│                                               │
│                                               │
└ ─ ─ ─ ─ ─ ─ ─ ─ ─ ─ ─ ─ ─ ─ ─ ┘
```

FORMULAS & ROUGH SKETCHES

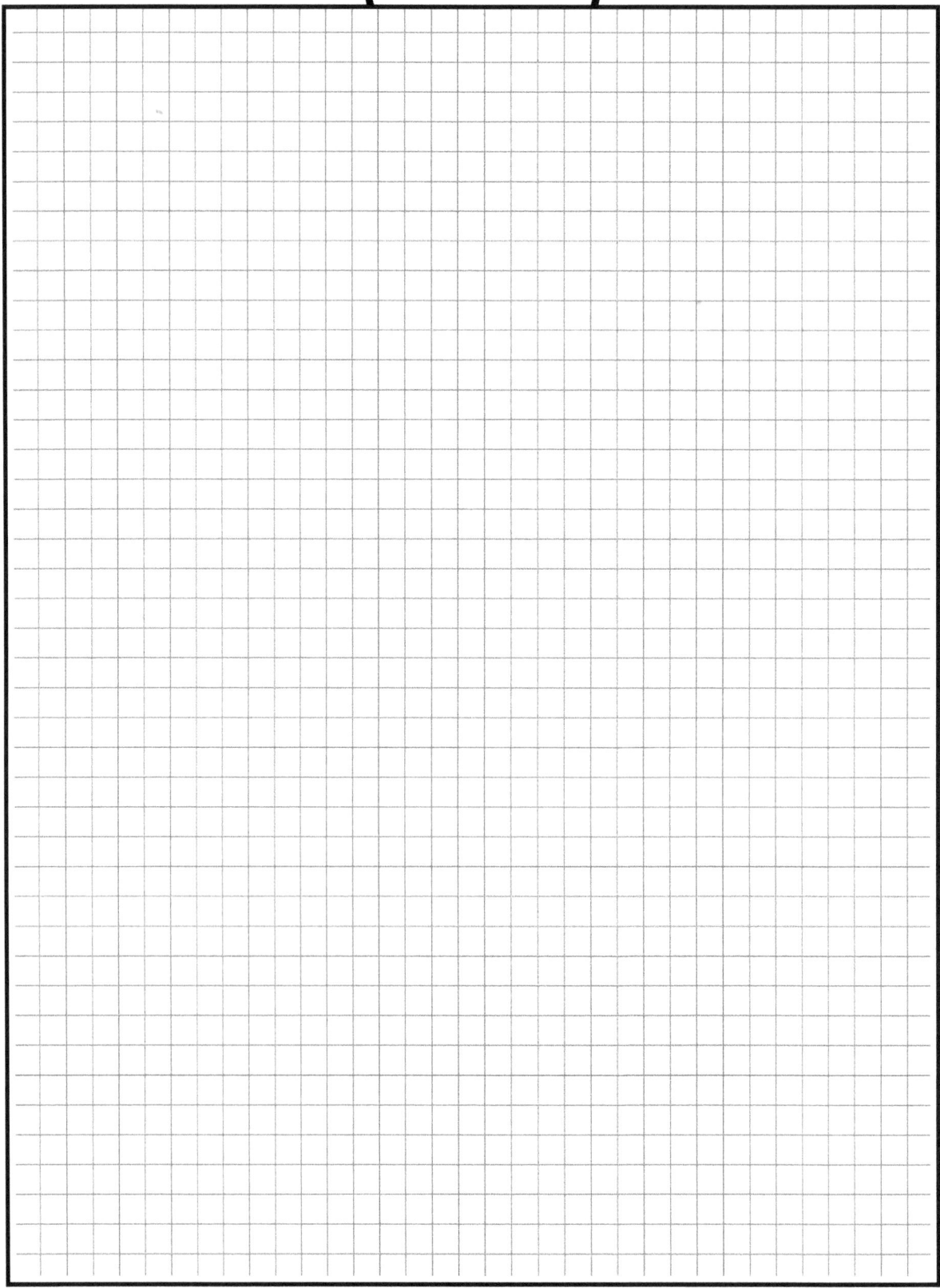

INVENTION

Description: _____

_____

_____

Designed / Created by: _____

Date created: _____

Where created: _____

Significance: _____

_____

_____

www.ingramcontent.com/pod-product-compliance
Lightning Source LLC
Chambersburg PA
CBHW081336090426

42737CB00017B/3174